THE FIRST BOOK OF
MARS

DISCARD

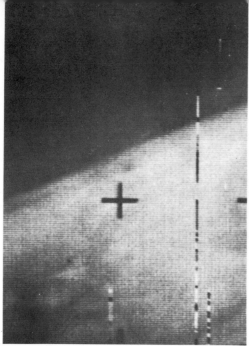

First photograph of Mars by Mariner 4

JPL technicians inspect Mariner spacecraft.

Old charts of Mars about 1910

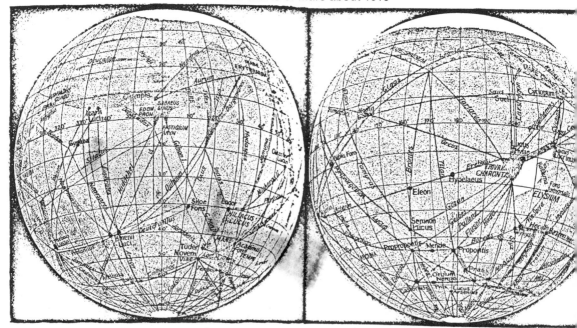

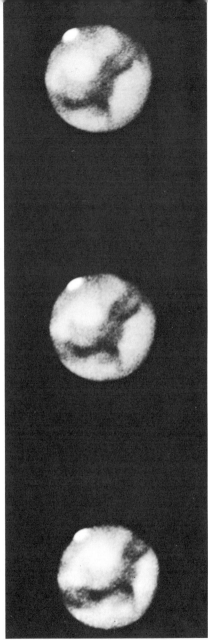

Atlas-Agena launches Mariner 4 on Mars probe.

Mars, rotation during 82 minutes

THE FIRST BOOK OF

MARS

DAVID C. KNIGHT

REVISED EDITION

AN INTRODUCTION TO THE RED PLANET

◄—A FIRST BOOK—►

FRANKLIN WATTS | NEW YORK | LONDON

*My thanks to Martin Steinbaum, formerly of
the Hayden Planetarium and presently
Planetarium Director of New Rochelle High School,
for his kindness in reviewing the manuscript.*

Cover design by Rafael Hernandez

Grateful acknowledgement is made to the various or-
ganizations and institutions who made illustration of
this volume possible: National Aeronautics & Space
Administration (NASA); The Bettmann Archive for the
illustrations from Wells' *The War of the Worlds;* The
Hayden Planetarium, New York City; United Press
International for material on the "Men from Mars"
broadcast of 1938; and of course to the following Ob-
servatories — Lick, Lowell, Yerkes, Mount Wilson, and
Palomar — whose staffs were particularly helpful with
astronomical material on the Red Planet. The front
cover color photograph and frontispiece of Mars, ©
Copyright 1959 by California Institute of Technology
and Carnegie Institution of Washington, is reproduced
by permission of Mount Wilson and Palomar Observa-
tories. Headlines for the Orson Welles radio broadcast
and Martian scare are copyright 1938 by the New York
Times Company and are reprinted by permission.
—D.C.K.

Library of Congress Cataloging in Publication Data

Knight, David C.
    The first book of Mars.

    (A First book)
    1. Mars. (Planet) – Juvenile literature. I. Title.
QB641.K55 1973   523.4′3   72-8123
ISBN 0-531-00797-9

CONTENTS

THE FIRST BOOK OF

MARS

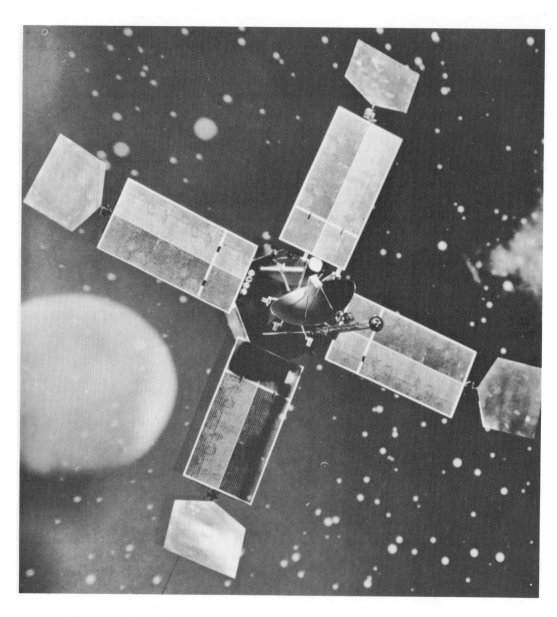

NASA's Mariner 4 spacecraft in simulated flight

DESTINATION MARS —
THE HISTORIC FLIGHTS OF
MARINERS 4, 6, 7, AND 9

Mariner 4

On Wednesday, July 14, 1965, the longest journey in the history of mankind was completed. To the scientists who had planned it — to the world who had watched and waited — it was a fantastic success. The incredible distance covered on this journey was more than 325 million miles. The time required was 228 days, or more than $7\frac{1}{2}$ months. The starting point had been the planet earth, November 28, 1964. The destination was a heavenly body of our own solar system, one that has fascinated man since the dawn of human history — the planet Mars.

The vehicle that made this fabulous trip was the Mariner 4 spacecraft. In so doing, it realized mankind's ancient dream of gaining firsthand knowledge about a neighbor in space. Mariner's flight was miraculous in two ways. First of all, it got there, passing within only 6,118 miles of the Martian surface. Secondly, during its "flyby," Mariner managed to send back, through millions of miles of space, the first closeup portraits ever made of the distant planet. Only three weeks before the powerful Atlas-Agena booster rocket had lifted Mariner 4 through the earth's atmosphere, Mariner 3 had failed in the same mission. So had Mariner 2 before it, while Mariner 1 had been sent on a similar (and successful) mission to Venus.

A space scientist's dream laboratory come true, the 575-pound Mariner 4 was crammed to capacity with complicated equipment. Inside its silvery eight-sided body made of magnesium and aluminum alloy, Mariner carried 138,000 components. Of these, more than 31,000 were electronic, ranging from a computer to a tiny $10\frac{1}{2}$-watt radio transmitter. The latter was designed to send back to earth a steady stream of reports on 39 scientific and 90 engineering measurements. Thus, while Mariner's primary mission was to obtain pictures of Mars, it also served an additional purpose by being equipped to transmit home valuable scientific information concerning cosmic dust, magnetic fields, the solar wind, and deep-space radiation.

Despite the ultimate success of Mariner's historic flight to Mars, not all had gone smoothly as it sped through space. Complex technical difficulties had to be overcome. Natural disturbances that spacemen call "glitches" had to be dealt with. When Mariner broke free from the booster-rocket stage, it unfolded the four solar panels that would power the instruments stowed within by converting the sun's energy into electricity. The panels shone with a bluish-colored glass which served to protect from harmful radiation the 28,224 solar cells that would accomplish this. And here was where the first trouble came.

Not sixteen hours after Mariner was launched, two solar pressure vanes — flaps attached to the ends of the panels — got stuck in the wrong position. This created a drag on the spacecraft which, unless corrected, would take Mariner hundreds of miles farther from Mars than planned.

There were other malfunctions, too. A defective metal clamp on the solar plasma probe equipment, installed to investigate solar wind energy, threw the apparatus out of adjustment. When a tube in the ionization chamber went dead, a power failure was created that put an end to the solar plasma experiment. Later, the ion chamber itself was put out of commission when a Geiger-Müller tube inside it "went delirious," perhaps because of a recent large flare on the sun.

A serious "glitch" developed when Mariner's roving navigation eye, or sensor, got "confused." The sensor had been set to track a star that would serve as Mariner's polestar to keep the craft on course. This was the bright, bluish-white star Canopus, but other bright objects began to attract Mariner's sensor. Once it "locked" on the wrong star for ten days until a command from earth redirected its attention to Canopus. On other occasions, a dust mote picked up in space distracted the eye by reflecting the sun's light.

A week after launch, when Mariner was 1.25 million miles out, it received its one and only trajectory correction from its masters on earth, the scientists at the California Institute of Technology's Jet Propulsion Laboratory (JPL), who were carrying out the Mariner program for the National Aeronautics and Space Administration. Not only did this correct for the drag created by the solar pressure vanes, but it also prevented the spacecraft from straying by many thousands of miles from its target — the Red Planet, Mars.

After this mid-course maneuver, a second correction was never needed. On February 11, JPL scientists decided to check out Mariner's all-important photographic equipment. The commands were given and all worked well. As a precaution, however, the JPL scientists decided then and there to remove the television camera's lens cover. Remembering the dust problems they had had previously, they decided that instead of waiting until the last minute, they would leave the cover off. If there was any dust on it, they did not want to risk its being shaken off at the crucial moment and "fooling" the sensors again.

Meanwhile, in spite of "glitches" and other difficulties, Mariner 4 was doing fine. Incredible distances were being covered and new records for space flight were being set. The spacecraft had already passed successfully through two streams of meteoroids after less than three and a half weeks of flight. Exactly one month after leaving the launch pad, Mariner passed the 50-million-mile mark; it had already made nearly 10 million separate scientific measurements of interplanetary space.

During the spacecraft's tenth week in flight, the earth moved ahead of Mariner; that is, the earth advanced in its orbit on a line drawn between Mars and the sun — and the planet would stay ahead of Mariner throughout the rest of its journey.

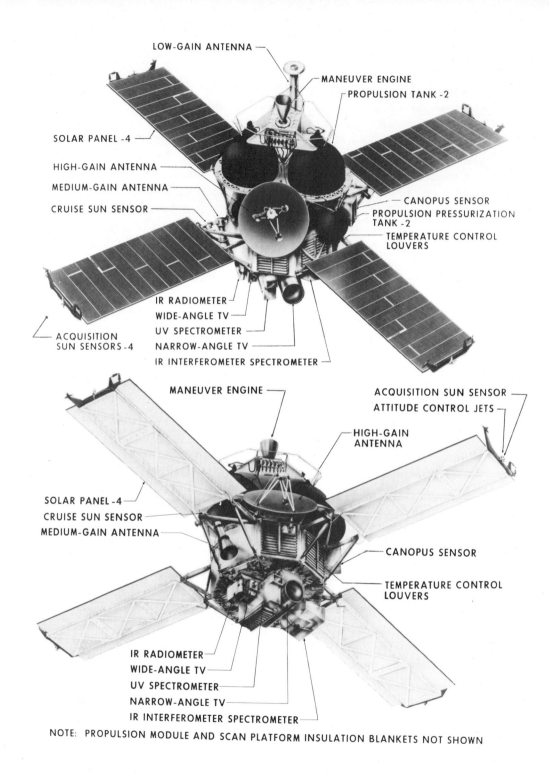

LOW-GAIN ANTENNA

MANEUVER ENGINE

PROPULSION TANK -2

SOLAR PANEL -4

HIGH-GAIN ANTENNA

MEDIUM-GAIN ANTENNA

CRUISE SUN SENSOR

CANOPUS SENSOR

PROPULSION PRESSURIZATION TANK -2

TEMPERATURE CONTROL LOUVERS

IR RADIOMETER

WIDE-ANGLE TV

UV SPECTROMETER

NARROW-ANGLE TV

IR INTERFEROMETER SPECTROMETER

ACQUISITION SUN SENSORS -4

MANEUVER ENGINE

ACQUISITION SUN SENSOR

ATTITUDE CONTROL JETS

HIGH-GAIN ANTENNA

SOLAR PANEL -4

CRUISE SUN SENSOR

MEDIUM-GAIN ANTENNA

CANOPUS SENSOR

TEMPERATURE CONTROL LOUVERS

IR RADIOMETER

WIDE-ANGLE TV

UV SPECTROMETER

NARROW-ANGLE TV

IR INTERFEROMETER SPECTROMETER

NOTE: PROPULSION MODULE AND SCAN PLATFORM INSULATION BLANKETS NOT SHOWN

On February 27, 1965, the spacecraft passed the 150-million-mile mark. By March 11, it had covered half the distance of the planned flight. It was a week later that the faulty ion chamber stopped sending back data altogether. On March 21, Mariner reached the halfway mark of its flight time.

From then on, nearly everything Mariner 4 did broke existing space records. On April 6, 130 days after launching, it broke the record of its sister spacecraft, Mariner 2, for the longest continuous operation of an American deep-space probe. On April 29 of the timetable, Mariner 4 set a new world's record for long-distance communication — its radio transmission had reached through 66 million miles of space to earth, exceeding that of the 1963 Soviet Union spacecraft called Mars I.

On May 12, Mariner had completed an astounding quarter billion miles of flight. Fifteen days later, it had reached a distance from the earth of 1 astronomical unit (au) — a span equal to the mean distance of the earth from the sun, which is about 93 million miles (although Mariner itself had really journeyed much farther).

Mariner sped on, through the rest of May, June, and then into July.

Encounter day, July 14, 1965, soon arrived — the day when Mariner's sensors were to start searching the sky for the planet Mars. The time was now past for the scientists back at JPL to test out thoroughly and correct any flaws in the delicate television and tape-recording equipment. This was because radio signals, even traveling at the speed of light (186,000 miles per second), would take some twenty-four minutes to make the round trip between Mars and earth. Still, there was time to send off four last-minute commands to Mariner, and these were dispatched — just to back up the programmed instructions already built into the apparatus. One of these, transmitted while the spacecraft was still about 107,000 miles from the planet, switched on Mariner's camera shutter mechanism, turned on the tape recorder's power, and started the wide-angled sensor searching for the sun's reflected light from Mars.

Top and bottom views of the Mariner Mars 1971 spacecraft

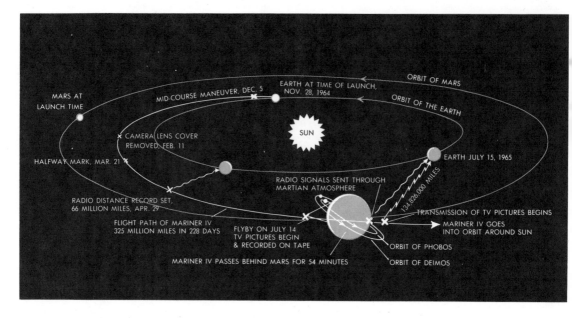

ORBIT OF MARS

MARS AT LAUNCH TIME

MID-COURSE MANEUVER, DEC. 5

EARTH AT TIME OF LAUNCH, NOV. 28, 1964

ORBIT OF THE EARTH

SUN

CAMERA LENS COVER REMOVED, FEB. 11

HALFWAY MARK, MAR. 21

EARTH JULY 15, 1965

RADIO SIGNALS SENT THROUGH MARTIAN ATMOSPHERE

134,826,000 MILES

RADIO DISTANCE RECORD SET, 66 MILLION MILES, APR. 29

TRANSMISSION OF TV PICTURES BEGINS

FLIGHT PATH OF MARINER IV 325 MILLION MILES IN 228 DAYS

FLYBY ON JULY 14 TV PICTURES BEGIN & RECORDED ON TAPE

MARINER IV GOES INTO ORBIT AROUND SUN

ORBIT OF PHOBOS

MARINER IV PASSES BEHIND MARS FOR 54 MINUTES

ORBIT OF DEIMOS

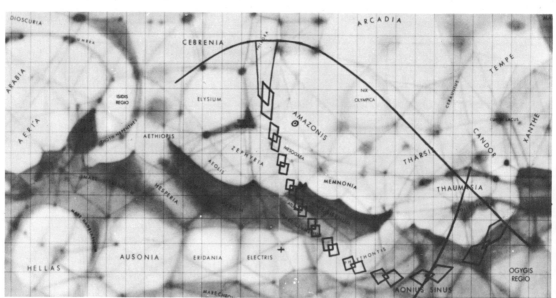

DIOSCURIA

ARCADIA

CEBRENIA

ARABIA

AERIA

ISIDIS REGIO

ELYSIUM

TEMPE

NIX OLYMPICA

AMAZONIS

CANDOR

XANTHE

AETHIOPIS

ZEPHYRIA

MESOGAEA

THARSIS

AEOLIS

MEMNONIA

THAUMASIA

HESPERIA

AUSONIA

ERIDANIA

ELECTRIS

AETHONIUS

OGYGIS REGIO

HELLAS

MARE CHRONIUM

AONIUS SINUS

It was about 5:00 p.m., earth time, when the first sensor picked up the *limb,* or edge, of the planet, and a few minutes later Mariner's television camera was recording its first picture sequences of the mysterious Red Planet.

It was 11:00 a.m., Martian time, when Mariner's cameras snapped the first photo at a distance of about 10,500 miles from Mars. There had been a slight miscalculation, however, and the spacecraft, now some 500 miles off course, was photographing the planet at a slightly different angle than planned.

Mariner's camera first focused on a 190-mile segment of the Martian region called Elysium in the northern hemisphere. The spacecraft then swept southeast, photographing as it went, over the eastern edge of an area known as Trivium Charontis. Continuing southeastward, more Martian regions with strange-sounding names were being caught by Mariner's camera — Zephyria, Mare Sirenum, Mare Cimmerium. Finally, its flight path narrowly missing the southern polar cap, Mariner swooped around the back side of the planet; that is, the side away from the earth.

Mariner 4 remained out of touch with the earth for some fifty-four minutes. But, as it performed this maneuver, the spacecraft carried out one of its most important experiments. This was to beam radio signals through the Martian atmosphere back to earth. There, scientists would be able to study the signal's changes in frequency and amplitude in order to get a clearer picture of what the Martian atmosphere is like.

When Mariner re-emerged from behind Mars, it was able to resume transmission of radio signals. Mariner's actual picture-taking time had only been about twenty-five minutes, but it would take at least eight days for the delicate equipment to play back the photo

Mercator projection of Mars (bottom left) shows areas photographed by Mariner 4. Longest line represents edge of Mars as viewed from craft during picture-taking period. Areas to right of lower curved line were in shadow. Photo #1 at top showed edge of Mars and blackness of space beyond. Photo #2 overlapped lower portion of #1. Photo #19 entered shadow line near Aonius Sinus. Circled dot near Amazonis is point where sun was directly overhead.

sequences to earth. In all, there would be twenty-one photos and part of a twenty-second taken of the Red Planet and stored on magnetic tape. Once played back and developed on earth, it would take scientists weeks of painstaking analysis to determine what was really shown.

When past Mars, its pictures taken, and the monumental job of experimenting completed, Mariner 4 curved into a never-ending orbit around the sun. A few weeks later, its radio signals, too weak to be picked up on earth any longer, faded out. Was Mariner now a useless blob of metal, a dead satellite perpetually orbiting about the solar system? Not at all. Scientists hope that when Mariner again comes within radio range of the earth, it will yield up more secrets now locked in deep space.

Mariners 6 and 7

The flights of Mariners 6 and 7 were quite similar to that of Mariner 4. Mariners 6 and 7 did, however, use a different launch vehicle. Instead of the Atlas-Agena booster rocket, Atlas-Centaur launch vehicles were used because of additional weight. Mariner 6 lifted off at 8:29 p.m. EST on February 24, 1969, and Mariner 7 was launched at 5:22 p.m. EST on March 27 of the same year. While Mariner 6 made the trip to Mars in 156 days, Mariner 7 made it in 130 days. The shorter length of time for Mariner 7 was due to the orbital motions of earth and Mars. Both required one mid-course correction, which had to be executed with extreme care. A mistake of one mile per hour in either case could have resulted in a 5,000-mile error when the spacecraft reached the vicinity of the Red Planet.

The outward trip of Mariner 6 went as planned. Although there were tremendous mathematical odds against it, Mariner 7 suffered a direct hit by a micro-meteoroid, which resulted in near disaster. When the particle struck Mariner 7, the blow caused the spacecraft to lose its "lock" on the star Canopus — its guidance reference or "fix." The next five hours or so were anxious ones for the ground controllers. Eventually they were able to stop the craft's tumbling and relock onto Canopus. This feat in itself was remarkable. The time factor was so tight that if the controllers had not executed the manuever at the precise moment they did, Mariner 7 would have had to be abandoned so that they could concentrate on Mariner 6, which was just entering the "near-encounter" phase of its flight.

Both spacecraft were heavier and more advanced versions of Mariner 4. Each carried six experiments, five of which were designed to yield data on the chemical, physical, and thermal nature of Mars and its environment. The sixth experiment was designed to yield astronomical data. After Mariners 6 and 7 completed their missions to Mars, like Mariner 4, they continued in solar orbit.

Mariner 9

On May 29, 1971, Mariner 9 began its 167-day, 248-million-mile journey to Mars atop an Atlas-Centaur launch vehicle. Its mission was to study Mars from many aspects for a minimum period of 90 days. It was injected into a Mars orbit on November 13, 1971. Because of the nature of its orbit, Mariner 9 will continue to circle the Red Planet for a minimum of 17 years.

Mariner 9 flight path to Mars. The spacecraft was inserted into Martian orbit so that it could photograph 85 percent of the planet's surface. It will retain its orbit around the Red Planet for at least 17 years.

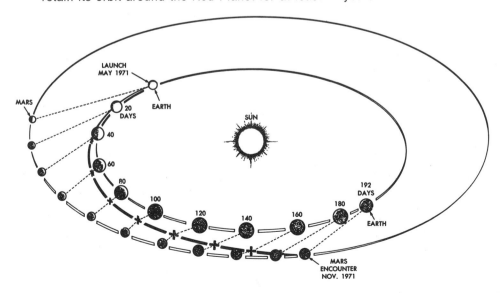

Mariner 9's mission was a multi-faceted one. Approximately 85 percent of the entire surface of the planet was photographed and some 7,000 photographs were radioed back to earth. The composition, density, pressure, and temperature of the atmosphere, as well as the structure, temperature, and composition of the planetary surface, are presently being studied at great length. Data on the changes in surface markings, such as the seasonal darkening observed from earth during the Martian spring, has also been obtained and is being evaluated. Earth scientists, in fact, have received so much data from Mariner 9 that the complete evaluation and analysis of all the material may take several years.

HOW THE MARINERS MADE
AND RELAYED BACK
THE FAMOUS PICTURES

When the Mariners' scanning sensors sight Mars, the photographic equipment is automatically turned on and a six-inch vidicon tube is focused on the planet through a reflecting telescope. The programmed mechanisms are set to take one photograph every forty-eight seconds. To provide information about the coloration of the Martian surface conditions, the pictures are alternately shot through red and green filters.

The camera used by Mariner 4 to photograph Mars was a television camera. Unlike commercial television screens, however, which are made up of some 525 scanning lines, each picture taken of Mars was made up of 200 lines. In turn, each of these lines was made up of 200 dots, or picture elements. Multiplying 200 by 200, each photo therefore contained 40,000 dots, or picture elements. For about twenty-five seconds, each of the 21½ pictures was held on the TV camera tube until each dot had been scanned by an electron beam designed to respond to the varying brightness of each dot. Next, each of these dots was translated into a numerical code; the shadings ran from 0 for an all-white area of the Martian surface to 63 for the blackest area "seen" by the vidicon tube.

These dot numbers had actually been encoded in the special "language" used by computers — the *binary,* or two-number, code, which uses 1's and 0's *only.* Each dot number was assigned six "bits" of information, composed of combinations of 0's and 1's. Thus, 0, or white, received the binary number of 000000, while 63,

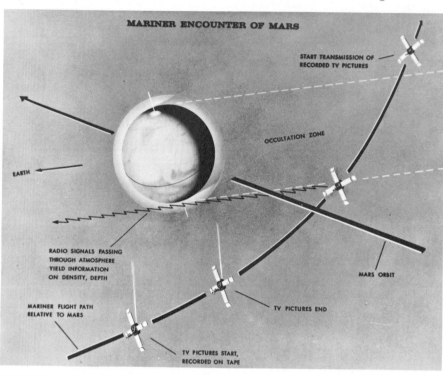

MARINER ENCOUNTER OF MARS

START TRANSMISSION OF
RECORDED TV PICTURES

OCCULTATION ZONE

EARTH

RADIO SIGNALS PASSING
THROUGH ATMOSPHERE
YIELD INFORMATION
ON DENSITY, DEPTH

MARS ORBIT

MARINER FLIGHT PATH
RELATIVE TO MARS

TV PICTURES END

TV PICTURES START,
RECORDED ON TAPE

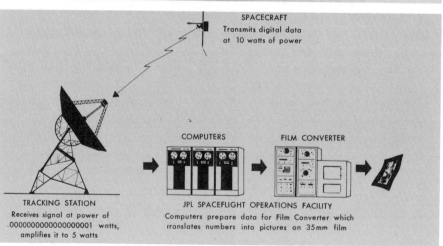

SPACECRAFT
Transmits digital data
at 10 watts of power

COMPUTERS

FILM CONVERTER

TRACKING STATION
Receives signal at power of
.0000000000000000001 watts,
amplifies it to 5 watts

JPL SPACEFLIGHT OPERATIONS FACILITY
Computers prepare data for Film Converter which
translates numbers into pictures on 35mm film

or black, was encoded as 111111. Any combination in between was a varying shade of gray. Each of the pictures that Mariner took — that is, 40,000 dots variously encoded as 240,000 "bits" (6 x 40,000) — was stored away on magnetic tape for transmission back to earth.

In Mariner 4's historic 25 minutes of picture-taking, it had collected 5 million "bits" of information which were eventually relayed back to earth by the tiny $10\frac{1}{2}$-watt radio transmitter. Due to the weakness of the signals and the great distance involved, it took as long as 8 hours 35 minutes to transmit back to earth the data that made up a single picture of the planet's surface. By the time the signals reached one of the tracking stations, they had been reduced to the incredible weakness of one billionth of one billionth of a watt!

But it was enough. Picked up by huge parabolic ("big dish") antennae at tracking stations around the globe, the signals were amplified or increased in strength a thousand times. Digit by digit — that is, "bit" by "bit" — they were received at JPL in California and reconstructed, or "developed," by computers to produce translated images of various shadings of the Martian surface on photographic film.

Mariners 6 and 7 far surpassed Mariner 4's ability to return data to earth. Mariner 4 had the capacity to transmit $8\frac{1}{3}$ bits per second. Numbers 6 and 7 had a high bit rate of 16,200 per second, and pictures containing more than three million bits (much more detail than the Mariner 4 photographs) were transmitted in mere minutes. Mariner 9's over 7,000 pictures covered about 85 percent of the surface of Mars. These pictures were of much higher quality than any of the ones from previous Mariner flights.

Bottom left, stages in Mariner 4's picture transmission and recording

WHAT THE MARINER PROBES "SAW"—
SOME IMPORTANT QUESTIONS
ABOUT MARS ARE ANSWERED

The new information revealed by the Mariner probes forced scientists to change their previous ideas about Mars. Other beliefs concerning that planet were confirmed. Briefly, here is what the historic flights revealed about Mars.

The magnetic field of Mars seems to be practically nonexistent. If it can be said to have any at all, it is only a tiny 1/1000 to 1/10,000 that of the earth's. This greatly surprised scientists, for it seemed to indicate that Mars (like the moon, which also lacks a significant magnetic field) has a different basic internal structure from that of the earth. Most scientists think that the earth's magnetic field is a result of the motion of a molten metallic core deep within it. This would imply that Mars, which lacks such a magnetic field, also lacks a molten metallic core.

Further, Mars does not show any evidence of having radiation belts around it similar to the earth's Van Allen belts. But this is perhaps to be expected, for a planet with no significant magnetic field cannot trap the charged particles that create such belts. Moreover, since the planet lacks a magnetic field to trap particles and since it has a very thin atmosphere, the heavy radiation from the sun directly bombards the Martian surface with a force many times greater than that at the earth's surface.

According to the information returned to earth by Mariners 6 and 7, the solid material on the Martian surface is of silicate origin. No evidences of vulcanism (volcanic activity) were found by Mari-

A Mariner 9 photo of Mars taken in November, 1971. The south polar cap shines dimly through the great dust storm. Picture was taken with craft's narrow-angle camera from a distance of 145,000 miles.

The 75-mile-wide crater enclosing smaller ones, with Atlantis between Mares Sirenum and Cimmerium, as photographed by Mariner 4 in the famous photo #11

Striking view of Mars taken by Mariner 9 on its 37th orbit shows the Phoenicis Lacus area — a relatively young region covered by volcanic deposits.

The Martian Nix Olympica (Snows of Olympus) region of Mars, an early photo taken by Mariner 9 showing mountain standing above the Martian dust storm

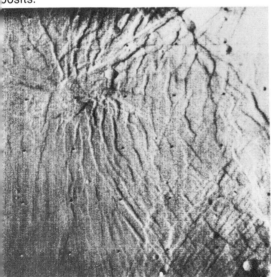

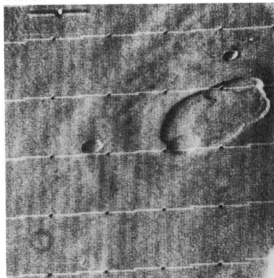

A Martian mountain near Nodus Gordii (The Gordian Knot). Crater shown measures 70 miles in diameter.

A 435-mile-long sinuous valley in the Rasena region of Mars. Photo was taken by Mariner 9 on January 22, 1972. This feature may be the result of the collapse of the roof over the subsurface lava flows or possibly the result of erosion of water far back in Mars' history.

A vast chasm with branching canyons eroding the adjacent plateaulands. Taken by Mariner 9 on January 22, 1972, the distance to Mars from the spacecraft was 1,225 miles.

Another view of Nix Olympica, a gigantic volcanic Martian mountain more than twice as broad as any on earth

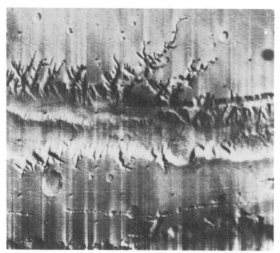

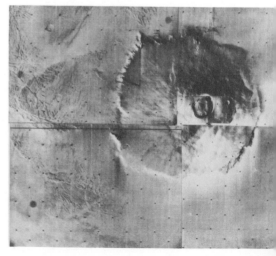

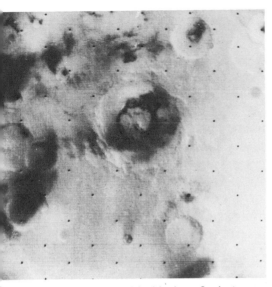

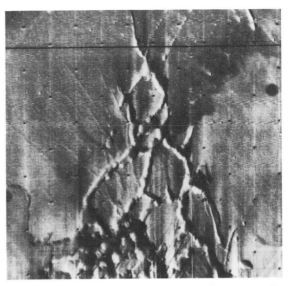

he dark splotches on this Mariner 9 photo are
the south temperate zone of Mars. Origin of
ese areas is not known. Crater at center, with
ng around its floor, is about 77 miles in diam-
ter.

Intricate network of mighty canyons appears to
hang like a gigantic chandelier from the Martian
equator (black line). It provides dramatic evidence of erosional processes at work on the
fractured volcanic tablelands of Mars' Noctis
Lacus.

A sinuous Martian valley photographed by Mariner 9. Valley is about 250 miles long and about
3 miles wide. It resembles an earth *arroyo*, or
water-cut gulley, indicating that there may have
been enough water in Mars' distant past to cut
such a feature. However, there is much dis-
agreement on this point.

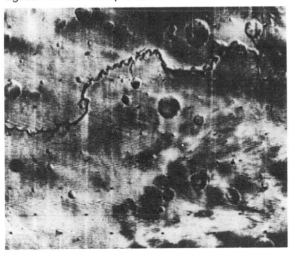

ners 6 and 7, but were definitely revealed in Mariner 9 photography. As predicted by astronomers, the planet Mars is essentially spherical with a very slight flattening at the poles. The radius measurement of Mars at its equator is 2,035.8 miles and 2,023.8 miles at 79° North Latitude. Neither Mariners 4, 6, nor 7 was designed to supply a definite answer to the question of whether there is life on Mars. In fact, no evidence gleaned during their flights indicated the presence of life. This, however, does not exclude the possibility.

When the Mariner 9 probe arrived at Mars and was inserted into orbit, it was apparent that there was an unexpected event taking place on the planet's surface. A great dust storm was occurring on Mars and most of the surface of the planet was obscured from the television eyes of Mariner 9 for the first 30 to 40 days. Scientists are of the opinion that such dust storms of this magnitude occur only about every fifteen years and that it was most fortunate Mariner 9 was there to photograph the event. The great dust storm gave scientists an unprecedented opportunity to study the dynamics of the Martian atmosphere. Some water vapor was found to be apparent in the Martian south pole region. Although the amount is only 1/1000 of what is present in the earth's atmosphere, it is to date the highest amount that has been detected on Mars. No evidence of any water vapor was found in the region of the northern polar cap.

The ultraviolet spectrometer experiment aboard Mariner 9 reinforced the information received by Mariners 6 and 7 that the upper Martian atmosphere is composed primarily of molecular carbon dioxide (CO_2) and that the temperature is much cooler than the upper atmosphere of earth and relatively constant. Atomic hydrogen and oxygen have also been noted in the upper Martian atmosphere.

Some of the conclusions reached after the flight of Mariner 9 are as follows:

1. The increase in knowledge about Mars derived from Mariner 9 was by a factor of 1000.

(18)

2. A more precise, spherical shape for Mars was determined, with slight flattening at the poles.
3. There is definite evidence of past vulcanism and possible evidence of present vulcanism as well.
4. Because of definite evidence of water vapor, there is a much improved chance of there being some form of life on Mars. But positive knowledge of this must await future probes or a manned landing on the planet.
5. There seems to be nothing revealed in the Mariners' photography resembling the famous "canals" on Mars. Hence, they must be presumed to be an optical illusion.
6. The Martian atmosphere near the planet's surface was warmer in 1969 (as recorded by Mariners 6 and 7) by about 20° Fahrenheit than it appears to be now (as recorded by Mariner 9). The upper Martian atmosphere is considerably warmer than that at the planet's surface.

When the early Mariner photos were developed, analyzed, and published, the scientific world was surprised. The Red Planet — the one planet in the solar system for which earthmen had held out hope for some sort of life — was apparently a dead world with a crater-pocked, lunar-like landscape.

Many of these historic photos turned out to be clearer and sharper than the scientists had expected. The pictures from Mariner 4 showed at least 70 clearly distinguished craters, ranging in diameter from 3 miles up to 75 miles.

Some of the craters in the Martian southern hemisphere appear to be rimmed with frost; others display what is thought to be frost inside some craters and possibly several frost-covered peaks. If this early sampling of the Martian surface is a representative one, scientists estimate that Mars may have at least ten thousand craters compared with fewer than two hundred still to be seen on the earth. Thus Mars, in showing these scars of ancient collisions, looks much more like the moon than the earth.

The first scientific interpretation of the craters was because they appeared so well preserved they must be very old — perhaps two to five billion years. This could only mean that little or no water erosion had taken place on Mars. The photos made by Mariners 4, 6, and 7 showed no evidence of such earthlike features as river valleys. Unlike the processes at work on earth, nothing seemingly had erased this record of ancient impacts on Mars — no water action, no mountain building, no piling up of sediments. Nor did the photos show definite continental outlines or ocean basins. From all this, scientists at first deduced that Mars may never have had a significant amount of water during its entire history; that its atmosphere may never have been much denser than it is now; and that, in fact, Mars may never have known rainfall and therefore never possessed any large bodies of water.

But a later analysis of the early Mariner photos has disputed this first interpretation. Some scientists now think that the surface age of Mars may be only a fraction of that first estimate and that erosion by dust storms, water, and other processes may have been widespread early in Mars' history. Why? Because the rate of crater formation on Mars should be about 25 times higher than that of the moon. This is due to the fact that Mars is closer to the asteroid belt (between Mars and Jupiter). Particles from the belt probably did most of the crater-forming. However, the Mariner photos show that the surface of Mars is pocked by only $1/6$ as many craters as would be expected if it were as old as some regions on the moon. Therefore, runs the new argument, the craters on Mars are only about a sixth as old as the lunar ones — between 300 and 800 million years. Because of this, scientists think it possible that much older Martian craters may have been worn away by erosional processes. In other words, stated one scientist, it is not impossible that "liquid water and a denser atmosphere were present on Mars during the first 3.5 billion years of its history."

Thirty or 40 days after Mariner 9's arrival at Mars the great dust storm began to clear. Among the surface features photographed by Mariner 9 were craters, calderas (collapsed central portions of volcanoes), fault zones, and great basins. Volcanic mountains, too, were photographed along with many other volcanic surface features, such as lava pits and volcanic vents.

One of the most significant photos transmitted to earth is one showing a spectacular channel. It is a very complex pattern and shows many little side-branching valleys that end up in feature-less areas. This channel is such that NASA scientists are hard put for an explanation of this feature other than running water. This feature may indicate that at one time there was indeed enough water to cut such a channel. This particular question has yet to be more fully investigated. There is no doubt scientists will find out more from continuing research.

MARS IN FOLKLORE
AND FICTION

Of all the planets in the solar system, Mars has stirred men's imaginations the most. It has remained the object of greatest popular interest because of the possibility of its supporting some kind of life.

Mars is one of the brightest objects in the night sky. To the unaided eye it appears even brighter than Jupiter, the giant among the planets. When it appears close to the sun at sunrise or sunset, Mars is sometimes called a morning or evening star. Mars is often called the "Red Planet" because its light, which is reflected sunlight, shines with a reddish or orange color. Due to the thinness of its atmosphere, Mars is the only planet whose surface can be more or less plainly seen with a telescope from the earth, with many of its features clearly identifiable. More has been written about Mars — both fact and fiction — than about any other planet; in fact, more has been written about it than all the other planets put together.

Mars was well-known among ancient peoples. Ever since the early Babylonians named it the Star of Death, it has been associated with bloodshed and disaster. Human sacrifices were made to Mars by the ancient Syrians. Choosing their victims for their "resemblance" to the Red Planet, the Syrian priests, clothed in red and smeared with blood, would offer a red-haired, red-cheeked man to Mars in a temple that was painted red and draped with red hangings. There is also evidence that the Egyptians performed similar rites to appease their gods.

Although there were other names for the planet before that, it was the Romans who named Mars for their bloody God of War. Mars has the symbol ♂, consisting of a shield and a spear. In turn, its two tiny satellites are named after the horses of the God of War — the Greek word Phobos (meaning "fear") and Deimos (Greek for "terror"). There is also an old superstition that speaks of Mars being in a certain prominent position in the night sky before every major battle ever fought in the world's history.

Because of the possibility of life on Mars, the planet was a favorite subject for writers of early science fiction. Especially after the discovery of "canals" by the Italian astronomer Giovanni V. Schiaparelli and the later observations of the American astronomer Percival Lowell (which we shall discuss later), imaginative writers of fiction poured out stories about "little green men," creatures as high as skyscrapers, and other fantastic beings who were conceived of as inhabiting the mysterious Red Planet.

One of the earliest — and best — of these fantasy writers was the prolific English novelist H. G. Wells. In 1898, Wells published a book called *The War of the Worlds* which described in highly realistic manner how Martian creatures with gigantic machines of destruction invaded the earth. Forty years later, an American actor and producer, Orson Welles, adapted a radio dramatization of Wells' old fantasy and proceeded to "scare the wits" out of the American people. Probably the most outstanding example of the Red Planet's hold on the public mind, the story of Welles' broadcast, and people's reactions to it, is worth describing here.

On Sunday evening, October 30, 1938, over the Columbia Broadcasting System, Orson Welles' Mercury Theatre Players gave a drama called "The Men from Mars." To make things more realistic, Welles arranged the play in the form of a series of news broadcasts. Interspersed with weather forecasts and hotel dance music, a voice interrupted these programs with a "flash" from a professor at "Mount Jennings Observatory," Chicago, who reported seeing ex-

Two illustrations from H. G. Wells' *The War of the Worlds.* Invading Martian robots create consternation as they sweep unchecked across Britain. Eventually the creatures inside the machines proved to be octopus-like and vulnerable and were defeated.

plosions on the planet Mars. Then listeners were "returned" to the dance music. Then further "news bulletins" were given that frantically reported the arrival of Martians in huge metal cylinders. "They" were landing in New Jersey. From this point on, the play gathered speed, with bulletin after frenzied bulletin being issued.

With the "defeat" of the New Jersey State Militia, the invasion by the Martians was reported to be going on all over the United States. Flamethrowers, heat rays, and other diabolical weapons were reported laying waste to the whole country. New York was being "evacuated."

Orson Welles and his Mercury Theatre Players rehearsing a broadcast of "The Men from Mars."

Model of a "machine from Mars" used in connection with the famous radio broadcast

Radio Listeners in Panic, Taking War Drama as Fact

Many Flee Homes to Escape 'Gas Raid From Mars'—Phone Calls Swamp Police at Broadcast of Wells Fantasy

A wave of mass hysteria seized thousands of radio listeners throughout the nation between 8:15 and 9:30 o'clock last night when a broadcast of a dramatization of H. G. Wells's fantasy, "The War of the Worlds," led thousands to believe that an interplanetary conflict had started with invading Martians spreading wide death and destruction in New Jersey and New York.

and radio stations here and in other cities of the United States and Canada seeking advice on protective measures against the raids.

The program was produced by Mr. Welles and the Mercury Theatre on the Air over station WABC and the Columbia Broadcasting System's coast-to-coast network, from 8 to 9 o'clock.

The radio play, as presented, was to simulate a regular radio pro-

Here is what the Martian "invasion" headlines looked like on the front page of the New York *Times* the day after the radio broadcast.

Radio listeners everywhere began calling up the police or the newspapers to find out what to do. In panic-stricken communities, people rushed out of their houses, milled about in the streets, and began to flee from what they thought was certain destruction. A woman in Pittsburgh, preparing to take poison, cried, "I'd rather die this way than that!" In Newark, some families, convinced that a "gas attack" had begun, wrapped their faces in wet cloths and began packing all their belongings into cars. A woman in a Midwestern city rushed into a church and screamed, "It's the end of the world. You might as well go home to die. I just heard it on the radio." Farmers began blockading the roads with anything they could find and stood guard over them with shotguns and pitchforks.

According to the radio version of H. G. Wells' fantasy, the "men from Mars" looked like this.

Orson Welles explaining to news reporters about the "war panic" broadcast

And so it went, all over the country, with women fainting, men grim-faced and waiting, everyone convinced that terror and mortal danger were close at hand.

The curious thing about the whole affair was that an announcer had clearly explained the nature of the program at the beginning of the broadcast. Also, it had been a scheduled program, the names used were fictional, and the program itself was even interrupted once to give a routine station identification. And, if panicky listeners had only twisted their dials a bit, they would have heard the reassuring voice of Charlie McCarthy, whose program was being aired at the same time as Welles'.

Actually, it is thought that this example of mass hysteria was caused by the uneasiness of those days. Welles' broadcast was given only a month after the Munich crisis of 1938. People's nerves had been shaken by Hitler, Mussolini, and the threat of impending war. Still, for a few hours at least, people's minds were dominated by the Red Planet.

Today, with the firsthand information that the Mariner probes have provided, the decades of dreaming, speculation, and science fiction concerning Mars have come to an end. For, if there is some sort of life on Mars, it is certainly not in the form of the creatures concocted by H. G. Wells' imagination.

MARTIAN FACTS AND FIGURES —
THE ASTRONOMY
OF THE RED PLANET

Mars' Position in the Solar System

Mars is the fourth planet out from the sun and revolves around the sun between the paths of Earth and Jupiter. Mars is quite a bit farther away from the sun than the earth is. While the mean distance of the earth from the sun is approximately 93 million miles, the figure for Mars is about 141 million miles. It is sometimes a little nearer or farther away than that.

Like the orbits of the earth and the other planets, the Martian orbit is an ellipse in shape. An ellipse looks like a circle that has been stretched slightly out of shape. As it happens, the orbit of Mars is more elliptical than that of the earth. Astronomers would say that the orbit of Mars is more *eccentric* (the more an ellipse departs from the shape of a true circle, the more eccentric it is said to be). Because of its more elliptical orbit, Mars' distance from the sun varies more than the earth's does. At *perihelion,* or the point in its orbit when it is closest to the sun, Mars is about 128,500,000 miles away from the sun. At *aphelion,* or its farthest distance from the sun, Mars is about 154,500,000 miles away from the sun.

How close does the Red Planet come to the earth — and when? Because the two planets are traveling at different speeds and in different orbits, the distance between the two can vary widely. Similarly, the points at which one overtakes another in their orbits varies widely with respect to time. Both planets travel around the sun in the same direction.

(29)

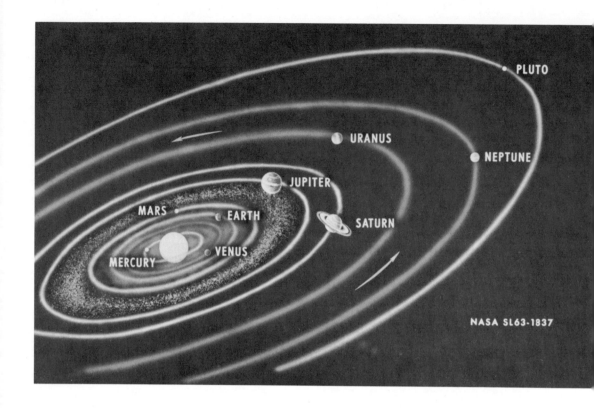

NASA SL63-1837

When Mars is said to be *in opposition* — that is, when Mars is on the other side of the sun from the earth (with the sun between the two planets) — the Red Planet averages a huge 234,400,000-mile distance from the earth.

Because it is an outer orbital planet, Mars is best seen from the earth when it is *in conjunction* — that is, on the other side of the earth from the sun — or when it is nearest us, with the earth between Mars and the sun. Oppositions of Mars occur every 780 days, or once every 2 years 50 days. Why? Because the earth, which travels around the sun at a faster speed than Mars does, overtakes and passes the slower-moving Mars once in the 780-day period.

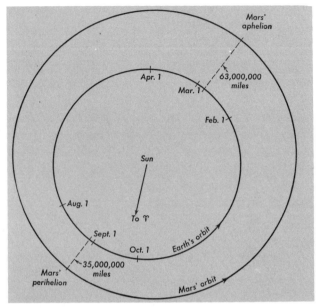

Diagram showing Mars at perihelion and aphelion

Two charts of Mars drawn one hour apart on June 4, 1888. Left one was drawn by Schiaparelli in Milan, Italy; right, by H. J. Perrotin in Nice, France. Differences are due to rotation of Mars during the hour interval, individual drawing styles, and the variations in perception and interpretation even between skilled observers.

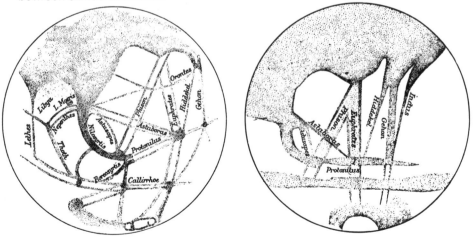

When this happens, the distance from Mars to the earth can range from as close as 34,600,000 miles to as far as 62,900,000 miles, depending on the point in the Martian orbit where the opposition occurs.

Thus, Mars comes closer to the earth in some years than it does in others. The most favorable oppositions occur at intervals of fifteen or seventeen years (as in 1939, 1956, 1971), and always in August or September, for the earth is nearest Mars' perihelion in late August. At such times, astronomers can study Mars in great detail. During the favorable opposition of 1956, scientists observed the planet closely, knowing that conditions would not be as favorable again until 1971.

Diagram showing past and future orbits of Mars and the earth

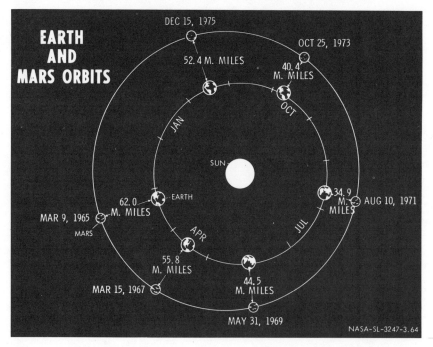

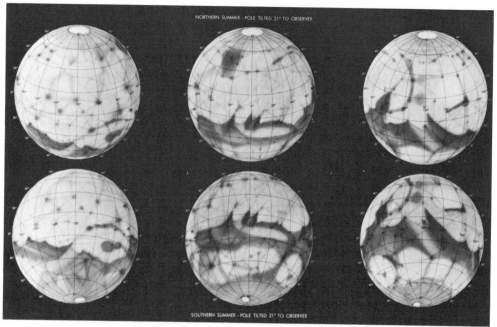

NORTHERN SUMMER - POLE TILTED 21° TO OBSERVER

SOUTHERN SUMMER - POLE TILTED 21° TO OBSERVER

Representation of northern and southern Martian summers with poles tilted 21° to an observer out in space. Actual tilt of planet is about 24°.

The Martian Day, Year, and Seasons

Useful telescopic observations of Mars extend back to the middle of the seventeenth century and have made possible a very accurate measurement of Mars' *period of rotation* — that is, the time it takes to spin, or rotate, once on its axis. The planet has been found to rotate eastward in 24 hours 37 minutes 22.7 seconds — a figure that is accurate to a few hundredths of a second. Just as on earth, this spin produces a cycle of day and night. As can be seen, the Martian day is very nearly the same length as an earth day, the Martian day being only 41.5 minutes longer than our own.

Mars travels along its orbit at about 15 miles a second (about 3.5 miles a second slower than the earth). It takes 687 of our days for

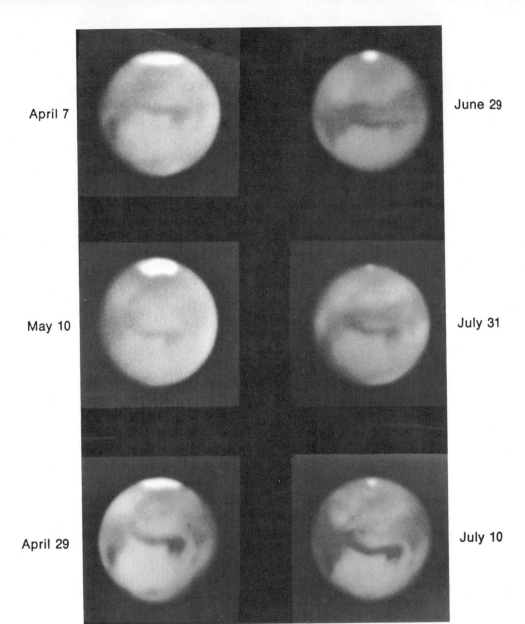

April 7

June 29

May 10

July 31

April 29

July 10

Mars photographed during its spring and summer, showing melting of southern cap and striking seasonal development of dark markings in the tropics. Note gemination, or doubling, of dark bands across center. Martian dates given correspond to earth calendar dates in Northern Hemisphere.

the planet to make a complete trip around the sun. Thus, a year on Mars lasts almost twice as long as a year on earth.

Mars also possesses another feature that is strikingly like the earth's — it has an axial tilt of about 24 degrees, as compared with the earth's 23.5-degree tilt. In the same way that this axial tilt gives the earth its seasons, so does the tilt of Mars' axis bring about the Martian seasons. But the Martian seasons are much longer than ours, since that planet takes almost twice as long as the earth does to orbit the sun. This means that each of the Martian seasons lasts nearly six earth months. In addition, whereas the earth's small variations in distance from the sun produce no noticeable effect on its seasons, Mars' much greater change of distance causes more extreme summers and winters in its southern hemisphere. It also makes the Martian seasons in that hemisphere more unequal in length — spring is 199 days; summer, 182 days; fall, 146 days; and winter, 160 days.

The Size of Mars

Compared with the earth, Mars is a small world. Figures vary, but the generally accepted one for the mean diameter of the planet is 4,140 miles, which is a little more than half that of the earth. As a result, the Martian surface area is a little more than a quarter of the earth's, and its volume is only about a seventh of our planet.

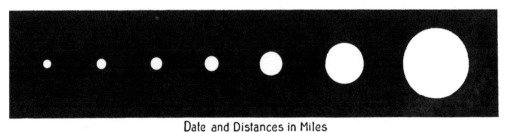

Date and Distances in Miles

Aug.12,1923	Oct.15,1923	Dec.15,1923	Feb.14,1924	Apr.15,1924	June 15,1924	Aug.22,1924
236,900,000	235,900,000	205,100,000	152,700,000	101,400,000	58,500,000	34,600,000

Changes in the apparent size of Mars. In August 1923, Mars was in conjunction and at its greatest distance from the earth. In August 1924, it was in opposition and closest to earth.

Like the earth, Mars is made up of rocklike material. Even if Mars were the same size as the earth, it would not weigh quite as much as the earth does. This is what scientists mean when they say that Mars is less *dense* than the earth. As calculated by astronomers, Mars is only about 70 percent as dense as the earth. The reason for this may be that Mars has a much smaller amount of iron than the earth does.

Since Mars is both smaller and less dense than the earth, it has a much weaker gravitational pull. The figure most often given for Martian surface gravity is .38, meaning that bodies or objects on Mars would weigh only 38 percent of what they do on earth. For example, a 100-pound earthman would weigh only 38 pounds on Mars; and, assuming that man suffered no ill effects from his journey and still had his normal muscular strength, he would be able to accomplish far more with less effort on Mars.

When a rocket is fired from earth, it must travel at about 7 miles per second before it can escape the earth's gravitational pull. The escape velocity for a rocket shot from the moon is only 1.5 miles per second. The escape velocity for Mars falls between these two figures. On Mars, a rocket would have to be traveling at a speed of about 3.2 miles per second to escape the planet.

Like the other planets whose orbits are outside that of the earth, Mars, as seen from the earth, does not go through a full cycle of phases, like the moon or Venus. It is noticeably gibbous, however, when it is at *quadrature* — that is, when straight lines drawn from the earth to the sun and from earth to Mars form a right angle. A planet is said to be *gibbous* ("humpbacked" or "lopsided") when more than half, but not all, of its disk can be seen.

Does Mars Have an Atmosphere?

It does. But after scientists studied Mariner radio signals beamed through the Martian atmosphere, they learned that it was extraordinarily thin — much more so than was previously thought.

Once scientists thought that the density of Martian air was about the same as that of the earth's at an altitude of around 60,000 feet. This figure was then revised upward to 80,000 feet. It was later re-

Artist's conception of how a spacecraft may someday be used to re-supply missions to and from Martian outposts

vealed that the air enveloping Mars is about as thin as that of the earth's at altitudes as high as 93,000 to 102,000 feet — or higher.

The average air pressure at the earth's surface is 1013 millibars. Not so long ago it was believed that the surface pressure on Mars was about 85 millibars. Then spectroscopic studies of Mars taken on earth reduced this figure to 25 millibars. Further studies made from the infrared light coming from Mars whittled this figure down to 10 millibars. Then, in March of 1965, an Aerobee rocket fired from New Mexico scanned the ultraviolet light coming from the Red Planet and, when the results were published, the surface pressure was declared to be from 5 to 20 millibars.

Now it appears, from the latest analysis of the Mariner data, that the lowest of these figures — a tiny 5 millibars — is in fact the air pressure at the Martian surface. In terms of pounds per square inch at sea level, this works out to mean that the atmospheric pressure on Mars is a very low .17, compared to the earth's hefty figure of 14.7.

Such extreme thinness of the Martian atmosphere would probably rule out the possibility of its supporting a winged vehicle or parachute, both of which have been considered for "soft-landing" instrument capsules on Mars. Landing the first probe on Mars will probably have to depend on other means, perhaps using braking-, or retro-, rockets. For, successfully landing a craft on Mars will require slowing it down from thousands of miles per hour to a speed low enough so that it can survive an impact with the Martian surface.

The atmosphere of Mars is mostly carbon dioxide (CO_2). Most of the early estimates of the percentages of the gases contained therein were made by *spectroscope,* an instrument that analyzes the light originating from or reflected by an object. The spectroscope reveals that Mars does have an atmosphere. By studying the make-up of this light, scientists can tell what gases probably make up the "air" of Mars. A few years ago, astronomers believed that the Martian atmosphere contained roughly twice as much carbon dioxide as our own. Later investigations reversed this — only a tiny amount of CO_2 was present after all. The best analysis before the Mariner probes was that the Martian "air" was mostly nitrogen; some estimates ran as high as 98 percent.

But now, taking into account the Mariner observations combined with the most reliable spectroscopic data, the gas that best fits a description of the Martian atmosphere is carbon dioxide. Scientists are now of the opinion that this gas must form most of the atmosphere of the planet, with only very small amounts of nitrogen and argon present.

Some observations have shown that there are small traces of water vapor in the Martian atmosphere. But this amount is very small compared with the plentiful supply in our own atmosphere. This brings up a question about the clouds that some observers have reportedly seen floating across the disk of Mars. They can hardly be water clouds, like those of earth, because there is not enough water vapor in the air to form them. One explanation is that they are dust or sand clouds raised from the planet's surface by strong winds.

If there is any oxygen on Mars, it must be a tiny amount indeed. Some studies have found slight traces of it; others have found none. Since this gas is vital for supporting the higher forms of earth life, its almost total absence in the Martian atmosphere must all but rule out life there as we understand it. But one thing is certain: future travelers to Mars must carry their own air supply with them if they are to survive.

By observing Mars through a good telescope, one can easily see just how sparse the Martian atmosphere is. As Mars moves through the night sky, any star passing behind it is very rapidly cut off from view. With planets having extended atmospheres, like Jupiter, they disappear much more slowly.

Temperature Variations on Mars

Because Mars is farther from the sun than the earth is, the Red Planet receives less light and other radiation than the earth does. Surface unit for surface unit, Mars has been estimated to receive an average of only 43 percent as much sunlight as our planet. As we would expect, therefore, Mars is quite a bit colder than the earth. Also, since the polar caps are seen to shrink and grow with the changing seasons, this would indicate that there are changes in temperature on Mars.

Because of the thinness of the Martian atmosphere, there is very little atmospheric blanketing. Heat radiates rapidly away from the surface. This makes for a high variation in the daily temperature range — 150°F. or so. The temperature falls rapidly after noon, and is probably below freezing every night. It has been estimated that the *maximum* temperature variations on the planet can range as widely as from 86°F. to as low as minus 150°F. But these are extremes.

Many measurements of Martian temperatures have been made by spectral analysis, and these vary. Generally speaking, however, when Mars is closest to the sun, the temperature at its equator is about 70°F. When farthest from the sun, the temperature at its equator is about 30°F.

In what corresponds to our Temperate Zones — halfway between the Martian poles and the equator — the summer temperatures range from about 30°F. to 70°F. In winter, the temperatures in these same areas range from about minus 20° to minus 60°F. In summer, the temperatures at the poles range from about 10° to 50°F. In winter, they may have temperatures from minus 110° to minus 150°F.

The Albedo of Mars

The percentage of light reflected from a planet's surface is called its *albedo,* after a Latin word meaning "white." The albedo of Mars is .15; that is, Mars reflects 15 percent of the light that it receives from the sun. The other 85 percent is absorbed and heats the surface. Area for area, the disk of Mars is more than twice as good as a reflector of light as either Mercury or the moon. It is far inferior to Venus, however, which has the highest albedo of any planet, .76.

THE SURFACE FEATURES
OF MARS

More than any other planet, the surface of Mars has been intensely studied both by eye and by photograph. Some features of its landscape are permanent, some appear to change, and some are regular seasonal phenomena. In the light of what knowledge has been gained from the Mariner probes let us look at some of the highlights of Martian geography.

The Polar Caps

The two surface features that astronomers can see most easily — provided the season is right — are the gleaming white polar caps of Mars. These are the large white areas at the north and south poles of the Red Planet. (See photos on next three pages.)

As Mars moves around the sun, its polar caps change from season to season. They are largest at the end of the Martian winter. At its maximum, a cap may cover some 4 million square miles. Sometimes the southern polar cap reaches nearly halfway to the Martian equator. In places, either one can creep equatorward to Martian latitudes as low as 40°, which, in terms of earth's latitude, would bring our northern cap as far south as New York, Rome, Madrid, or Chicago. The south polar cap of Mars gets both larger and smaller than the north polar cap, a fact that clearly indicates the more ex-

Next three pages show successive photos taken of Mars from July through October during the favorable opposition year of 1956. Note waning and waxing of polar caps.

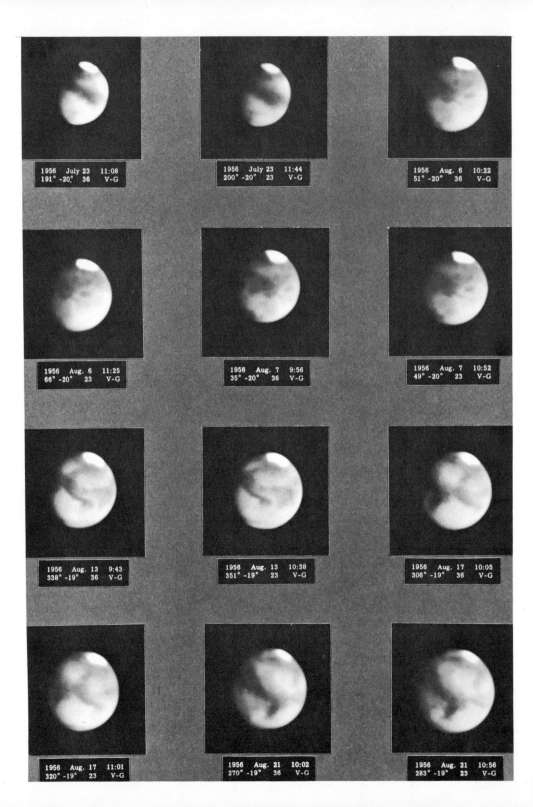

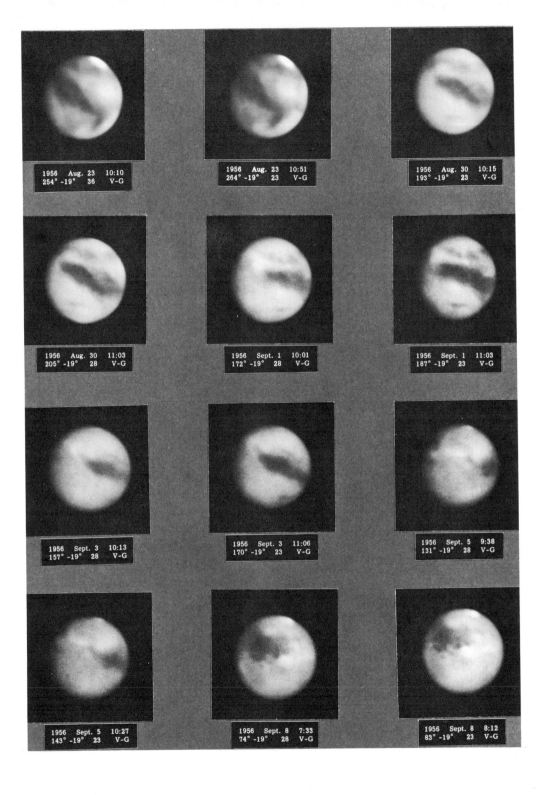

1956   Aug. 23   10:10
254° -19°   36   V-G

1956   Aug. 23   10:51
264° -19°   23   V-G

1956   Aug. 30   10:15
193° -19°   23   V-G

1956   Aug. 30   11:03
205° -19°   28   V-G

1956   Sept. 1   10:01
172° -19°   28   V-G

1956   Sept. 1   11:03
187° -19°   23   V-G

1956   Sept. 3   10:13
157° -19°   28   V-G

1956   Sept. 3   11:06
170° -19°   23   V-G

1956   Sept. 5   9:38
131° -19°   28   V-G

1956   Sept. 5   10:27
143° -19°   23   V-G

1956   Sept. 8   7:33
74° -19°   28   V-G

1956   Sept. 8   8:12
83° -19°   23   V-G

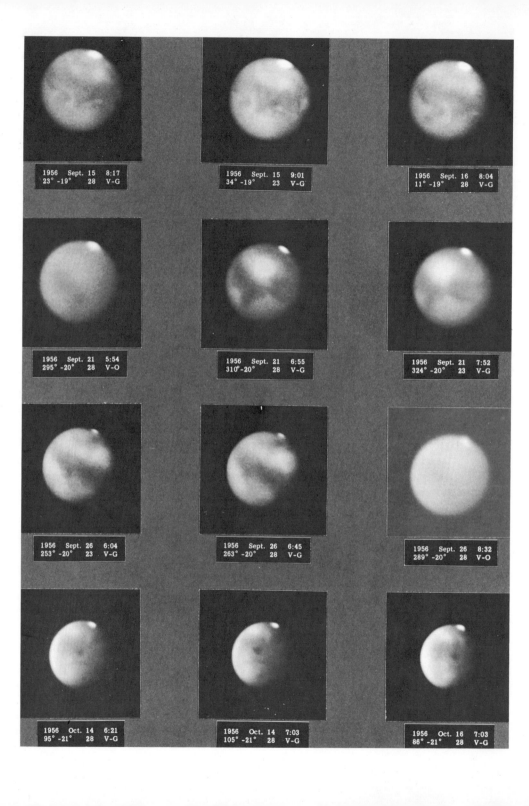

1956   Sept. 15   8:17
23° -19°   28   V-G

1956   Sept. 15   9:01
34° -19°   23   V-G

1956   Sept. 16   8:04
11° -19°   28   V-G

1956   Sept. 21   5:54
295° -20°   28   V-O

1956   Sept. 21   6:55
310° -20°   28   V-G

1956   Sept. 21   7:52
324° -20°   23   V-G

1956   Sept. 26   6:04
253° -20°   23   V-G

1956   Sept. 26   6:45
263° -20°   28   V-G

1956   Sept. 26   8:32
289° -20°   28   V-O

1956   Oct. 14   6:21
95° -21°   28   V-G

1956   Oct. 14   7:03
105° -21°   28   V-G

1956   Oct. 16   7:03
86° -21°   28   V-G

treme climatic conditions in this hemisphere. (Incidentally, most published photos of Mars show the southern cap as "up" rather than down; this is because the image of Mars that astronomers usually see in their telescopes appears upside down.) During some years the southern cap has wholly vanished; the northern cap, though it becomes very small, never entirely disappears.

As the Martian spring equinox approaches, the caps begin to shrink along their edges and recede poleward. By the end of summer they have almost disappeared. In the autumn, the caps begin to form again, growing larger as fall gives way to winter. During late spring and summer, each cap wanes in almost the same way, shrinking and splitting at the same time. The typical rifts and fragments probably indicate surface features of different levels, the last to disappear being colder and higher. In part, the Mariner probes bear this out, for some of the photos taken in the southern hemisphere indicate bright areas that are thought to be frosted peaks.

What is this white material that the Martian polar caps are made of? Certainly they are not great blankets of thick ice like the ones that cover our own poles, for there is not that much water vapor available in the Martian atmosphere. One theory is that they are frozen carbon dioxide — dry ice.

The Light Areas

As viewed from the earth, approximately three-quarters of the surface of Mars appears as a bright reddish, orange, or yellowish color. Unlike the dark areas of the planet which are seen to alter their shape, the light-colored areas do not seem to change. These areas are thought to be vast desert-like tracts, for the nature of the light reflected from them suggests that it is a mixture of silicates colored by mineral impurities and a powdered iron oxide known as limonite. One theory states that over the centuries, violent dust or sand storms may have been blown about by the winds of Mars, perhaps obscuring some of the surface features.

Although the surface of these desert and semidesert regions has been thought to be smooth, the Mariner photos reveal a vastly different story. At a distance of 8,900 miles, Mariner 4 photographed one of the light-colored areas known as Zephyria. Mariners 6, 7, and 9 also photographed this area. On these photographs a number of smaller craters appear. These photos are representative of Martian "desert" areas. It does not appear that constant wind erosion has taken place; otherwise, sand, dust, and other debris would long ago have filled up and erased these small craters.

Some authorities have attempted to explain the redness of Mars by the fact that its atmosphere contains little or no oxygen. They hold that the rocky surface material contains a certain amount of iron and that this has been oxidized — that is, combined with the oxygen of the air. According to this theory, the Martian rocks have captured far more of the oxygen of the atmosphere than have the rocks of the earth, and what we see is a "rusted" (oxidized) planet. While it has been neither proved nor disproved, this theory would account both for the redness of Mars and the scarcity of oxygen in its atmosphere.

The Dark Areas

Approximately the remaining quarter of the Martian surface consists of the so-called dark areas. Concentrated for the most part in the vicinity of the equator, these are the regions of Mars that have interested scientists the most. They are not of one uniform color and have variously been described as blue, green, brown, gray, and black. They are about half as bright as the desert areas.

Through a telescope these regions look like great patches hundreds of miles wide. Schiaparelli and other earlier observers thought that these dark areas might be water-filled basins, such as seas and lakes. Fanciful names were given to supposed seas (in Latin, *maria*), bays, lakes, channels, and swamps by their discoverers. Some examples are the Sea of Venus, Lake of the Sun, Bay of Pearls, Gulf of Arabia, Fountain of Youth, Bay of the Dawn, and so forth. But repeated failure to observe any bright flashes of reflected sunlight

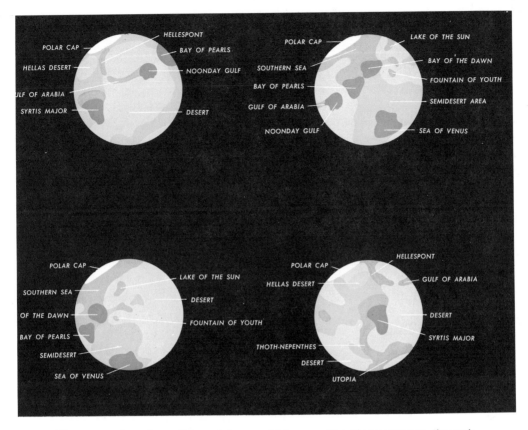

Diagrams show four different faces of Mars as the planet rotates through one day. Note fanciful names of dark areas assigned by their various discoverers. In diagrams, south polar cap is "up."

from them eventually ruled out the possibility that they were bodies of water.

Further evidence that they were not seas or lakes lay in the fact that the dark areas were observed to change both their shape and their color from time to time. The changes appear to be of two kinds. In one kind, the changes are seen to take place over a long period of time. With the passing of many years, a dark area may so radically change its shape that it no longer looks like the same area. Then, mysteriously, it may change back to its original shape again. One area in particular, The Lake of the Sun, is well-known for its change-ability.

Most of the dark areas, however, do not change this much, but keep their general contours like the bright areas do. Perhaps the best known of these is a dark area called Syrtis Major, which looks something like India in shape and projects well into the northern hemisphere. In 1659, Syrtis Major became the first feature discovered on Mars. Its outlines can be recognized in sketches of the planet's disk made by the scientists Robert Hooke and Christian Huygens more than three hundred years ago. By watching Syrtis Major astronomers can measure Mars' speed of rotation with great accuracy. Incidentally, a dark band arching down from Syrtis Major to a grayish area known as Utopia was once classified by some observers as one of the famous Martian "canals," which we shall learn about later.

The second type of change in the dark regions of Mars takes place over a shorter period of time — with the seasons. Some observers say that during the Martian springtime they see some dark areas turn to light green. In summer certain areas may seem to turn darker green. In the fall and winter, others appear to turn yellow and brown. A few astronomers, Percival Lowell among them, claimed that they observed such changes regularly. Others say that they have never been able to see any color changes at all.

Another curious color change takes place during each Martian spring. At the time of the shrinking of the polar cap in either hemisphere, areas near the retreating cap begin to darken and press toward the equator at the rate of about 50 miles a day. Ultimately some of these darkening areas cross into the opposite hemisphere. The effect is as if some form of vegetation were coming to life and spreading equatorward. To scientists, the baffling thing about this is that it is the opposite direction of the advance of spring on

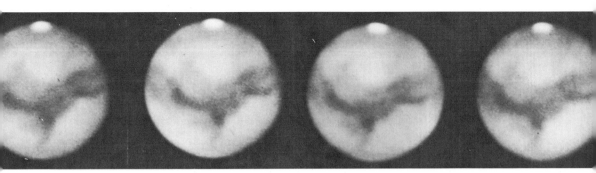

Four views of Syrtis Major taken in September 1909

the earth. For us, spring with its greenery advances from the equator and spreads toward the poles.

Certain authorities have believed that these springtime dark areas represent concentrations of a low form of plant life — perhaps moss or lichens. Also, various proposals have been made as to how such darkening could occur by nonliving processes — for example, cinder deposits from volcanoes — but none of them have been widely accepted. Even after the Mariner flights, this spring darkening is as much of a mystery as ever.

Shadows, Slopes, Craters, and Clouds

From studies of the photos taken by the Mariners, indications are that there are few steep slopes on the surface of the Red Planet. This is what one would expect of a planet which, unlike the earth, has not been shaken and torn by powerful internal forces.

The Mariner surface photos indicate that the craters have rims rising a few hundred feet above the surface of the planet and that central depths may reach a few thousand feet. Craters like these are typical of those produced by explosive impacts, an example of which is the famous Meteor Crater in Arizona. It was formed when a meteorite, or perhaps a small comet, struck the surface with such force that it exploded. The craters on the moon are generally of this type.

Also like those craters seen on the moon, picture number 11 taken by Mariner 4 showed a giant crater 75 miles wide, with a number of sharply defined, younger craters inside it. These large craters are very old. It is believed they are relics of a time when our solar system was much more cluttered with large-sized objects than it is today.

As we have already seen, one possible explanation why Mars has so many moonlike craters is that its orbit is near that of the asteroid belt. This belt consists of thousands of miniature planets and chunks of rock in orbit around the sun. Ancient collisions by these planetoids with the surface of Mars possibly account for the many craters "seen" by the Mariners.

What about the clouds that observers have occasionally reported floating over the surface of Mars? Are they illusions or real? During the missions of Mariners 6, 7, and 9, some very high frozen carbon dioxide clouds were noted and photographed. But since there is very little water vapor in the atmosphere, it is doubtful that atmospheric clouds, as we know them, exist.

THE PYGMY SATELLITES
OF MARS

Mars has two tiny satellites, or moons, in orbit about it. Curiously enough, they were objects of interest even before their discovery during the last century. In 1610, the famous German astronomer Johannes Kepler reasoned that Mars might have two satellites. However, in Kepler's day, there were no telescopes powerful enough to be able to see them. Yet so sure was Kepler of this that he wrote to the great Italian scientist Galileo of the probability. The French author Voltaire, in one of his imaginative works, also mentions Mars as having two moons.

But the most incredible anticipation of the two Martian satellites was made by the English writer Jonathan Swift in his famous *Gulliver's Travels,* published in the 1720's. In one of Gulliver's adventures, "A Voyage to Laputa," the two Martian satellites are described with a fair amount of accuracy. According to the story, the astronomers of Laputa (an island that was supposed to float above the earth) "discovered two lesser stars, or satellites, which revolve around Mars, whereof the innermost is distant from the center of the primary planet exactly three of its diameters, and the outermost, five; the former revolves in the space of ten hours, and the latter in twenty-one and a half." Actually, Swift's estimates were too great, for Phobos is only 1.4 times the Martian diameter away from the center of the planet, and the distance of Deimos is only 3.5 diameters. Swift's periods of revolution were off, too, as we shall see. Nevertheless, his guesses were astonishingly accurate, considering the fact that the little satellites were not actually discovered until one hundred and fifty years later.

(51)

Asaph Hall, discoverer of the two Martian moons, Phobos and Deimos

The discoverer of the two Martian satellites was Asaph Hall, an American astronomer working at the United States Naval Observatory in Washington, D.C. He was using a 26-inch refracting telescope, then the best one in existence. Hall, a master carpenter who had used his trade to get an education in astronomy, discovered the tiny Martian satellites in 1877, a year during which there was a very favorable opposition of Mars. On the night of August 11, Hall sighted a faint object near the planet. But cloudy weather intervened and he did not see it again until the sixteenth. Because it was seen to be moving with the planet, there was no doubt in Hall's mind that it was a satellite. The next night he succeeded in locating an inner satellite. Hall named the inner satellite Phobos and the outer Deimos, after the mythological horses that pulled the chariot of the god Mars.

Since Asaph Hall first saw the moons of Mars, other astronomers have studied the two satellites. It has been found that they orbit the planet from west to east, which is the usual pattern for most satellites in our solar system. The two satellites are very small in comparison with their *primary,* or parent, planet, and they are also very close to its surface.

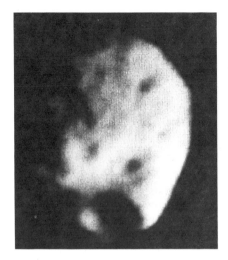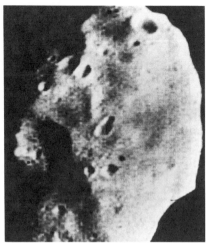

Left, this is man's first detailed view of Phobos, the inner satellite of Mars. The most spectacular feature is the 4-mile-wide crater seen at the top of the photo. This photo, taken by Mariner 9, reveals that Phobos is the rougher of Mars' small satellites. Right, this extremely detailed image of Phobos was taken by Mariner 9. The abundance of craters indicates that this innermost satellite of Mars is very old and possesses great strength.

Phobos

Phobos, the inner Martian satellite, is closer to its primary than any other known satellite in our solar system. It is only about 5,820 miles from Mars' center, which means that its distance from the planet's surface is only some 3,750 miles.

Phobos is a tiny world. Astronomers believe it is only some 10 or 12 miles in diameter. Because Phobos is so small, scientists have had to calculate its size from the amount of sunlight that it reflects. Small as it is, however, a person on Mars would be able to see Phobos quite easily. It would be seen as a disk in the Martian sky. And, just as our moon does, it would be seen to go through phases; that is, its shape would change from time to time. As seen from Mars, Phobos would have only one-third the diameter of our full moon and be only one twenty-fourth as bright.

Phobos travels around Mars very quickly. It takes the satellite only 7 hours 39 minutes to complete one orbit about the planet. Because Mars is spinning on its axis at a slower rate than this, Phobos travels around its parent planet faster than Mars itself rotates. Phobos is unique in that it is the only planet in the solar system to do this. Thus a person on Mars would see Phobos rise in the west and set in the east *three times* every Martian day.

Phobos' present short period of revolution is a result of the fact that it seems to be approaching Mars. Astronomers think that some 4.5 million years ago it probably had a period of about seventeen hours. The chances are that in another 35 or 40 million years it will end its life, either by breaking apart under the gravitational pull of the parent planet, or by crashing into Mars as a solid lump of rock.

Deimos

The outer Martian satellite is Deimos. It is even smaller than its sister, Phobos. Deimos has a diameter of only about 5 or 6 miles. A person on Mars would not even see this miniature world as a disk. It would look more like a bright star. As seen from Mars, Deimos would have only one twenty-fourth the diameter of our full moon, and it would be only one-fortieth as bright at Phobos.

Deimos is much farther from Mars than Phobos. It is about 14,600 miles distant from the center of the Red Planet. Deimos takes 30 hours 18 minutes to orbit Mars once. In other words, it revolves around its parent planet only a little more slowly than Mars itself rotates on its axis. Thus, Deimos would seem to rise reluctantly in the east and set slowly in the west. In fact, so slow is Deimos' motion across the Martian sky that before it sets the little moon remains in the sky for more than 60 hours. By comparison, Phobos takes only 4 hours 30 minutes to cross the Martian sky in the opposite direction. Unlike Phobos, Deimos is slowly receding from the parent planet instead of approaching it.

Most of the Martian year, the two little satellites would be visible only in the morning or evening twilight, for they would be either

Mars as seen from its outer satellite, Deimos. A painting by Howard Russell Butler

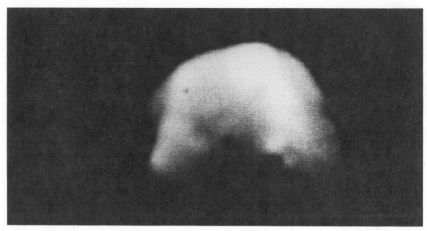

This is the first detailed view of Deimos, Mars' outer satellite. Note the two large craters along the terminator, the region of shading toward the right separating the day from the night side of the satellite. Deimos is about $7^1/_2$ miles high and about $8^1/_2$ miles wide.

invisible against the daytime sky or obscured by the shadow of Mars. Only in midsummer or midwinter would they avoid the parent planet's shadow long enough to be seen to make an entire trip across the sky. By comparison with our own moon (itself one of the smaller bodies in the solar system), the masses of these two small satellites are tiny indeed. Their gravitational attractions must be so feeble that an earthman of average weight would weigh only a few ounces on either satellite.

Where Did Phobos and Deimos Come From?

Astronomers are puzzled about the two miniature Martian satellites. Their extremely small size and closeness to the parent planet are hard to explain. How did they get there and where did they come from?

One explanation is that they are captured asteroids. As we know, asteroids, or planetoids as they are sometimes called, are small rocky pieces of matter that circle the sun between the orbits of

Mars and Jupiter. It may have been, during the early history of Mars, that the planet was able to capture the two little satellites as they came within its gravitational pull. If this is what Phobos and Deimos are, Mars may have more tiny objects in orbit around it which are too small for us to see.

Another theory suggests that both the Martian satellites and Mars itself were formed from material thrown off from the earth. Some $4^1/_2$ or 5 billion years ago — contends this theory — the earth was spinning on its axis much faster than it does today. A day may have been no more than three or four hours long. Because at this time the earth's crust had not yet hardened, the theory states that the earth threw off some of its material. Part of it became our moon, part of it became Mars, and part of it became Phobos and Deimos. The great depression left on our globe from the loss of this ejected material is the basin occupied by the Pacific Ocean. This theory, however, has not been proved true or false; it is most probably false.

Still another theory is one that seems almost pure science fiction. Yet this imaginative idea was seriously proposed as late as the year 1960 by a Russian scientist named Shklovsky. Briefly, Shklovsky's theory poses the question: What if Phobos is not a solid object at all, but hollow? Suppose it is, in fact, an artificial satellite launched into orbit by intelligent beings long ago? Because it is hollow, even the thin Martian atmosphere would be able to slow it down by atmospheric drag. This, as we know, is what is happening to Phobos — and why Shklovsky thinks it is an artificial satellite. He also thinks that Deimos may be one, too. There is, moreover, a good reason, Shklovsky suggests, why the two satellites were not discovered until 1877. They had not yet been "launched" by the Martians!

Fascinating as this idea may be, it of course presupposes that there were intelligent creatures who were capable of an advanced technology living on Mars at least a short time ago. But there is no evidence after the Mariner trips. Nor has science yet succeeded in explaining the presence of the pygmy Martian moons.

(57)

THOSE MARTIAN "CANALS"

Perhaps no subject in the whole field of outer space has captured the imagination of the world more than that of the so-called Martian "canals." Even after the early Mariner probes, some people still did not give up hope that they existed. The story of how they aroused the interest of millions of people is worth telling. It largely centered around the work of two astronomers, one Italian, the other American.

The Work of Giovanni V. Schiaparelli

Mars leaped into the headlines in the year 1877 because of an especially good opposition. It was during this year that Asaph Hall discovered Phobos and Deimos at the Naval Observatory in Washington, D.C. It should be emphasized, however, that even during a favorable opposition year, Mars, because of its small size, is no easy object to see. Assuming you have perfect viewing conditions, a good opposition year, and a very powerful telescope, the image of the Red Planet you would see is still only roughly equivalent to a small marble on the palm of your outstretched hand.

Early sketches of Mars by various astronomers show great variations in what these men thought they saw. Galileo, looking through his small telescope in the 1600's, glimpsed a Mars that he reported was all one color, with no markings on it. Some time after this, another Italian astronomer, Gaetano Fontana, made the first sketch of Mars. It showed a round, dark spot in the center of the planet, surrounded by a grayish ring; it may have been the result of eyestrain, although the center spot could possibly have been the most

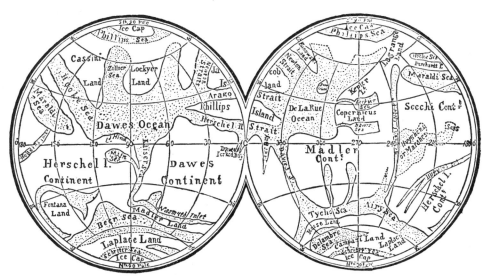

Map of Mars prepared in 1867 by Richard Anthony Proctor, English astronomer and writer. Note surface features named after earlier scientists.

conspicuous marking on Mars, namely, Syrtis Major. Later observers, with better telescopes, were able to make out bright regions and dark regions, assuming that the former were land areas and the latter, seas. During the late 1700's, the English astronomer Sir William Herschel, with a much improved telescope, was able to make out the more prominent markings on Mars. As the instruments got even better, astronomers saw more and more markings on the planet, and many fanciful "maps" of Mars began to appear. One is shown opposite that was prepared by an English astronomer, Richard Anthony Proctor, in the year 1867. In his map, Proctor acknowledges the work of earlier colleagues by generously naming surface features after them — Herschel Island, Fontana Land, Hooke Sea, Huyghens Marsh, and so on.

A few years before Proctor drew his map, a young astronomer in his late twenties was appointed director of the Brera Observatory in Milan, Italy. Giovanni Virginio Schiaparelli was to hold this position until his retirement in 1900. In 1861 he discovered the as-

The Italian astronomer, Giovanni Schiaparelli, who first saw the "canals" of Mars

teroid Hesperia. His later work included studies of double stars, cometary orbits, and meteor swarms. But it was in the year 1877 that he published his first famous accounts of the markings on Mars that he chose to call *canali*. Unfortunately, this word got translated into both French and English as "canals." The proper English translation of *canali* would be "channels." It was this mistranslation that helped start the whole "canal" story, for the word *canal* conveys the idea of an artificial waterway constructed by intelligent beings. But even people who were familiar with the Italian language disregarded the error. The thought of having found another inhabited planet was too exciting.

What had Schiaparelli actually seen through his telescope? He believed that he saw many thin, dark lines on the planet's surface. They were first observed as a network of fine lines or streaks upon the reddish or light areas. Unlike rivers or streams, which curve this way and that in their courses, Schiaparelli's "canals" followed perfectly straight paths. Some of these channels were plainly visible, while others were so fine that they could hardly be seen. They were thought to range in width from 20 to as much as 200 miles.

And that was not all Schiaparelli saw. Although the clarity with which he could see them varied trickily from week to week, the canals seemed to intersect one another at all kinds of angles. At these intersections there were usually small dark areas, which Schiaparelli thought might be "lakes" or some sort of artificial bodies of water. Although he was quite cautious about what he said concerning the *canali,* Schiaparelli then believed that the dark areas of Mars were seas and the light areas deserts. Every canal seemed to originate and end in what was thought to be a sea, lake, or another canal — none of them broke off in mid-desert. Schiaparelli himself wrote of the *canali* that "their singular aspect, and their being drawn with absolute geometrical precision, as if they were the work of rule or compass, had led some to see in them the work of intelligent beings."

With ideas about Mars filling people's thoughts and imaginations at this time, it was not long before the public jumped to certain conclusions. Unlike the earth whose seas covered nearly three-fourths of the planet, Mars was three-quarters land. Thus, water must be quite scarce on Mars. What could have been more logical than that the thrifty Martians should have covered their vast land areas with a network of canals, which met in lakes, to irrigate their desert regions?

Schiaparelli made a second set of observations during the opposition of 1877. This time Mars was farther away, but it was better situated above the horizon for observational purposes. At that time he observed several more canals, which were much finer than those he had sketched on his previous charts. Schiaparelli was also the first to note another peculiar effect of the canals. Some of them underwent a process called *gemination*, which means "to double." Two parallel canals were seen to appear where only one had been before.

Meanwhile Schiaparelli's reports of the Martian surface features had reached the ears of a young American who was uncertain what to do with his future. And the story of the Martian canals now shifts to the United States.

The Work of Percival Lowell
(1855–1916)

Born into a prominent Boston family in 1855, Percival Lowell spent much of his boyhood reading books on astronomy and observing the heavens with a small telescope that he set up on the family rooftop. Graduating from Harvard in 1876, Lowell spent the next five years in the family business in Boston. Shrewd investments made him sufficiently wealthy so that he was able to travel for several years in the Orient. Fascinated with the East, he spent ten years there, mainly in Japan and Korea, and wrote several books about his travels. Meanwhile, he had also become intrigued with Schiaparelli's reports concerning the "canals" of Mars. When he returned to America he renewed his study of astronomy and mathematics. He had learned that Schiaparelli's eyesight was failing and, since this would prevent the Italian astronomer from continuing his observations further, Lowell determined to continue them himself.

Needing an observatory, Lowell promptly had one built at Flagstaff, Arizona, where the atmosphere was especially steady and clear for observing the heavens. Dedicated to the study of the planets, Mars in particular, the Lowell Observatory was opened in 1894. By this time, seventeen years had gone by since Schiaparelli's observations of 1877, and it was now the year of another close opposition of Mars.

The famous American astronomer, Percival Lowell

After Lowell completed his 1894 observations at Flagstaff, he described them in the Observatory's *Annals;* he also wrote about them in his book called *Mars.* Lowell confirmed these first observations in the opposition of 1905 and expressed essentially the same conclusions in another popular book entitled *Mars as the Abode of Life.*

Lowell's first reports stated that " . . . we have proof positive that Mars has an atmosphere; we have reason to believe this atmosphere to be very thin — thinner at least by half than the air upon the summit of the Himalayas — and in constitution not to differ greatly from our own." Lowell also believed that the polar caps were frozen water, and that the average temperature on Mars was a fairly livable 48° F. During the Martian summer, Lowell concluded, the caps melted and the frozen water was released in liquid form. He also reached another conclusion, one that was shared by a fellow American astronomer, W. H. Pickering of Harvard Observatory. This was that the so-called *maria*, or "seas," of Mars (that is, the dark areas) were not seas at all, as Schiaparelli had thought, although they may have been the basins of real seas in the dim past. Now they were "generally, at least, areas of vegetation; from which it follows that Mars is very badly off for water, and that the planet is dependent on the melting of its polar snows for practically its whole supply."

As for the canals, Lowell described them as " . . . a network of fine, straight, dark lines. The lines start from points on the coast of the blue-green regions, commonly well-marked bays, and proceed directly to what seem centers in the middle of the continent, since most surprisingly they meet there other lines that have come to the same spot with apparently a like determinate intent. . . . The lines appear either absolutely straight from one end to the other, or curved in an equally uniform manner. There is nothing haphazard in the look of any of them . . . each line maintains its individual width, from one end of its course to the other . . . their length is usually great, and in cases enormous."

As for the intersecting points where the canals met, these now became known as "oases." Such small dark areas, wrote Lowell, "constitute so many hubs to which the canals make spokes." And, where Schiaparelli had only seen canals in the bright areas, Lowell, Pickering, and other observers now reported that they cut through the dark areas as well.

Writing in his popular book *Mars,* Percival Lowell summed up his conclusions as follows.

We find, in the first place, that the broad physical conditions of the planet are not antagonistic to some form of life; secondly, that there is an apparent dearth of water upon the planet's surface, and, therefore, if beings of sufficient intelligence inhabited it,

Various sketches of Mars and its systems of "canals" made by Percival Lowell. Note Syrtis Major in middle sequences.

(64)

12 35 <u>41 - 50</u> 11⁵ʰ a
12ʰ. 25ᵐⁱⁿ occⁿ 5

11ʰ 45 + 12 15
sketch

11 <u>15 - 24</u>
occⁿ 6+

Feb 5

Feb 6.

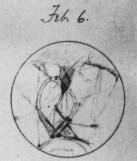

11ʰ <u>to</u> 11ᵗᵒ 45 →
sketch. —

10ʰ <u>45 - 11ʰ 45</u> occⁿ 6
orange glass 55ᵐ 24" apu.

11ᵗ 55 + 12 25 - 35
15" + 15½"

Feb 8.

9ʰ <u>10 - 40</u> occⁿ 7.
15?

they would have to resort to irrigation to support life; thirdly, that there turns out to be a network of markings covering the disk precisely counterparting what a system of irrigation would look like; and, lastly, that there is a set of spots placed where we should expect to find the lands thus artificially fertilized, and behaving as such constructed oases should. All this, of course, may be a set of coincidences, signifying nothing; but the probability points the other way. As to details of explanation, any we may adopt will undoubtedly be found, on closer acquaintance, to vary from the actual state of things; for any Martian life must differ markedly from our own.

Irrigation, unscientifically conducted, would not give us such truly wonderful mathematical fitness in the several parts of the whole as we there behold. A mind of no mean order would seem to have presided over the system we see — a mind certainly of considerably more comprehensiveness than that which presides over the various departments of our own public works. Party politics, at all events, have had no part in them; for the system is planet-wide. . . . Certainly what we see hints at the existence of beings who are in advance of, not behind us, in the journey of life.

And so the whole tragic, wonderful story developed and grew in people's imaginations. Its appeal was widespread and curiously intense. Here were a brave but helpless people, fighting a heroic but hopeless rearguard action against an environment so hostile that it must eventually wipe them out. A perhaps once-great and proud civilization was now fighting for its life — and slowly losing its battle to the inexorable forces of nature. For some reason, the planet had long ago begun to lose its water supply and, with the passing of the years, was drying up. The process was already far advanced, and the gallant Martians were using all their ingenuity to eke out survival for a few more years.

Over the centuries, as their little world became colder and drier, the people of Mars had had to move closer to the equator. Eventually their seas and lakes dried up entirely. The problem facing the

Martian engineers was how to convey the remaining small water reserves from their sources in the polar caps to the habitable equatorial regions. They solved it by building a monumental network of artificial waterways to carry the precious liquid down from the poles; as the caps melted in the spring, the water entered the canals and began to flow equatorward. The whole economy of the planet was now geared to conserving and making maximum use of the scanty water supply that remained. The Martian engineers, supposedly men of great skill, created a vast pumping system that forced this meltwater through the canals and beyond the equator. In this way, the springtime darkening at the rims of the caps was explained satisfactorily, for it was there that water caused vegetation to flourish first, and then spread from pole to equator. Actually, Lowell pointed out, it was these swaths of vegetation along the canals that we see from earth, and not the canals themselves. Oases, like those in our own deserts on earth, flourished as one canal met and joined another.

Additional touches were added that made the tragic tale even more poignant. For example, the whitish clouds sometimes seen by observers near the limb, or edge, of the planet, shining by reflected light from the sun, were interpreted as signals of distress by the hapless Martians. Another conjecture was that, since the nights on Mars must be uncommonly cold, the enterprising Martians had built their cities underground. Or, the swaths of vegetation along the canals really hid elaborate systems of highways along both sides of the waterways. Who really knew what lay hidden under the vegetation? Perhaps the Martian cities were built in long strips astride or along the canals, unlike our own circular cities that developed from an original center.

Any imaginative person can easily supply the ending to this story. Conditions on the Red Planet slowly grew worse and worse for the parched and shivering population. The old ones died off. Cities became ghost towns, and the howling Martian winds blew through abandoned streets. One by one, the pumping stations stood idle; it was useless to man them further for the thin trickle that now came from the dwindling caps. Young adults, barely able to sustain themselves, refused to leave their children the same legacy — and so the population dropped lower and lower. These Martians lived out their lives, died, and then there were none. Only the magnificent canals remained as silent testimony that there had once been intelligent life on Mars.

Today no one believes such a story as suggested by the writings and observations of Schiaparelli and Percival Lowell. But the controversy about the canals raged on for years. A number of astronomers confirmed the markings seen by Lowell, while other observers, having just as good equipment and observing conditions, such as Edward E. Barnard in the United States and E. M. Antoniadi of France, were not able to see such detail. On the other hand, the Swiss-born astronomer, R. J. Trumpler, of the Lick Observatory, supported Lowell's views. So the dispute continued between those who could see the Martian canals and those who could not.

Why cannot a photograph, taken under the best of conditions, either confirm or deny the canal-like markings on Mars? The answer is that observations like those of Lowell's cannot be objectively checked by photography. While a photograph can show some of the more distinctive channel-like features on the planet, the exposure time required to bring out any more detail than this is longer for a photographic plate than it is for the moments of good seeing by the human eye. In other words, a photograph cannot reproduce the fine details that the eye can glimpse during an instant. This is why Schiaparelli, Lowell, and others had to make sketches of what they saw instead of photographing the planet's disk through their telescopes. Also, it is a known fact that the human eye will tend to bridge the gaps between faint details and, if such details are committed to paper, the drawer will tend to connect them up as a continuous, straight line. This may have happened in Lowell's case when he drew his charts of Mars.

Nor should it be forgotten that the best conditions under which Mars can be observed from earth are limited to a few months every

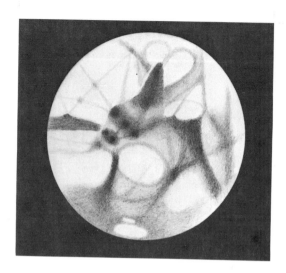

Chart of Mars drawn by
R. J. Trumpler in Septem-
ber of 1924

two years. Even then, the best view one can obtain of the Red Planet is little better than that of the moon seen with low-powered binoculars. Furthermore, most of the Martian surface features are accessible to observation for no more than two weeks continuously. And, since Mars has a slightly longer day than ours, the hemisphere that it presents to the earth is always fading slowly from view at any given hour as seen from the earth. Thus, if one is trying to observe a particular marking on Mars, that observation could be interrupted for nearly a month. In fact, to observe a complete cycle of the Martian seasons under the best conditions would take several years to accomplish. Under such difficult circumstances, it is small wonder that some of Lowell's fellow astronomers could not confirm his description of the surface features of Mars.

In the more recent studies of Mariner's photos, several apparent straight-line features have been discovered in some of the pictures. So faint are these "lines" that they escaped scientists' notice until fairly recently. Yet at best, any relationship between them and the so-called "canals" has been reported as "uncertain," and the conclusion of the scientists' is that the "canals" are presumed to be optical illusions as viewed from earth.

BUT IS THERE LIFE
ON MARS?

The chances of there being life on the Red Planet appear slim indeed. With each new discovery that science makes about Mars, the conditions for it grow less and less friendly. The grim crater-pocked surface, which is extremely dry and cold, suggests that the planet is as lifeless as the moon. Since Mars shows few signs of ever having possessed water, the chances of any kind of life there are considerably reduced. Most scientists agree that water is essential to the origin of life within the solar system.

Certainly no "Martians" inhabit the planet. Nor could any of the higher forms of earth-type life exist there. There are two very good reasons for this. First, the atmosphere is so thin it can scarcely prevent the sun's intense ultraviolet radiation from mercilessly striking the Martian surface. These rays would be enough to destroy all known types of even tiny earthlike life-forms. The thinness of the Martian atmosphere, combined with the absence of any magnetic shielding like the earth's, means that Mars also receives the full force of cosmic rays, which are believed to be high-energy atomic nuclei arriving from interstellar space. While these rays are stopped and made less intense in the upper layers of our own atmosphere, there is nothing to prevent them striking Mars and creating — so some scientists think — a layer of radioactive material hostile to life a few inches off the planet's surface.

Second, if the Martian atmosphere does contain mostly carbon dioxide, this condition alone would prevent the existence, as we know it, of living organisms. While CO_2 is not toxic (poisonous) in itself, its abundance in the Martian air to the exclusion of the breath of life as we understand it — oxygen — would cause living animals to suffocate. While the young earth was itself believed to be once rich in carbon dioxide, scientists think that the CO_2 combined chemically with substances in the oceans and lakes, from whence terrestrial life is assumed to have arisen. When primitive plants began to appear on the earth, they began to consume the CO_2 and, through a complicated process known as photosynthesis, generated oxygen into the air. Thus, the earth's once-abundant carbon dioxide was slowly subtracted from the atmosphere over billions of years and the oxygen level began to rise. As it did so, more complicated forms of life began to evolve upon the earth.

But apparently this has not happened on Mars. Its atmosphere today seems similar to that of the earth's some two billion years or more ago. The fact that Mars still has so much CO_2 suggests that life may never have been at work there. And the one agent that could have changed this state of affairs — water, in abundance — may not have been present to do so. As the Mariner photos show, there appears to be an absence of heavy water-erosion, indicating that oceans have not existed on Mars, at least not for a very long time.

Despite all this evidence against the case for life on Mars, some scientists still cling to the hope that it will turn up. As JPL scientists had anticipated, the Mariner photos were not expected to demonstrate the existence or nonexistence of life. One obvious setback, of course, was that if Martian oceans had never existed, then the search for a fossil record laid down by various sediments would not be a promising one. Yet it may be, as some biologists seriously suggest, that isolated "pockets" or small "oases" in which life could have arisen will be found on Mars.

Thus, the answer to this ancient riddle still eludes earthmen — and will continue to do so until space probes are actually soft-landed on Mars and the search for life begins in earnest.

MARS AS THE
FUTURE ABODE OF LIFE —
THE RED PLANET'S DESTINY

From what man now knows about Mars, including the possibility that there is no life there, he and the planet he lives on stand unique in the solar system. For only on the planet earth were conditions apparently just right for the emergence of intelligent life. This does not mean, however, that Mars — a planet not as fortunate as the earth — cannot be of future use to earthmen. It can — in more ways than one.

Even though the Red Planet never, so to speak, "made it on its own," it could still hold some of the secrets of the earth's own evolution. If the Martian surface is truly in a primitive stage, it may prove to be the best — perhaps the only — place in the solar system still preserving clues to original organic development — traces of which have long since disappeared from the earth itself.

Already plans are underway for sending an "automated biological laboratory" to Mars, which would land, take samples, monitor any biological events that may possibly be taking place, and send the information back to earth. But the technical problems involved in such a project are many. Before they are solved, additional space vehicles will probably be placed in low orbits around Mars. Previously, scientists thought that such a spacecraft could be placed in orbit around Mars no closer than 600 miles from the surface; otherwise, it was feared the craft might ultimately succumb to atmospheric drag and crash into the planet, carrying with it possibly contaminating microbes from earth. But now, with the Mariner probes' data

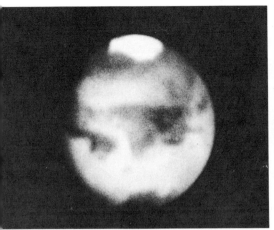

Opposite hemispheres of Mars, photographd during the planet's closest approach to earth in 1956. View at left was taken in orange light; right, in red.

reporting an extremely thin atmosphere, it is thought that a space vehicle would be able to remain in orbit almost indefinitely at heights as low as 100 miles.

As far as the near future of Mars is concerned — that is, the next several decades — what will be the role of the Red Planet in the lives of earthmen? Probably it will be a time of cautious and careful scientific investigation. Teams of scientists and astronauts will eventually establish bases and live there for weeks and possibly months, taking their own air supply with them, and possibly going underground to establish larger complexes as time goes on. Geologists will study the craters and other surface features, and dig into the surface to determine the structure of the planet. Biologists will use all the means at their command to scour the planet for possible signs of life, or places and conditions under which life might have arisen. Astronomers will establish an observatory whose telescopes, peering through the thin Martian atmosphere, will be able to probe farther into space than from earth. Probes will be launched from Mars to investigate conditions on Jupiter, Saturn, and the other

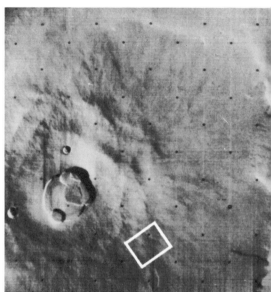
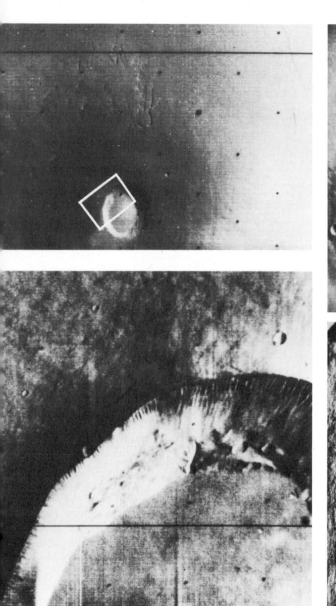

outer planets of the solar system. In all of these projects, extreme precautions will be taken against contaminating Mars with any terrestrial microbes that could destroy a truly unique opportunity to study the origins of life itself.

Looking further into the future, it is possible that the day will come when these scientific investigations will have been largely completed. By that time, scientists, astronauts, and other technical workers on Mars would already have brought their families out from earth and, for all practical purposes, would be inhabiting the planet as Martians. Some of their children would have been born on Mars, thus making them true natives of the Red Planet. As colonists, these men and their families could be considered the first wave.

Back on earth, it is highly possible that populations would have expanded to the danger point. Similar colonies on the moon may not have been able to handle the overflow. In short, the time will have come to colonize Mars in earnest. This will mean a vast and costly expansion of all living space and facilities on that planet. As more and more volunteers come out from earth, great subsurface cities will have to be constructed to accommodate them. As the decades pass, the colonists will come to accept the Martian way of life. They will have adapted themselves to whatever governments and political situations may prevail in that future time. People will be born, live out their lives, and die on Mars, perhaps never having visited the home planet earth. For them, Mars will be home.

Left, photo shows two views of a probable Martian shield volcano. It was taken on January 11, 1972, by Mariner 9 after the great dust storm had subsided. The smooth crater floor, which meets the wall abruptly, is probably a former lava lake. On January 7, 1972, Mariner 9 took these photos (right), five minutes apart, of the Nix Olympicus region. The feathery texture and elongated lobes suggest flowage of material downslope and away from the central crater complex. A raised ridge, with an irregular crack remaining along its crest, can be seen. These features are similar in appearance to terrestrial lava flows.

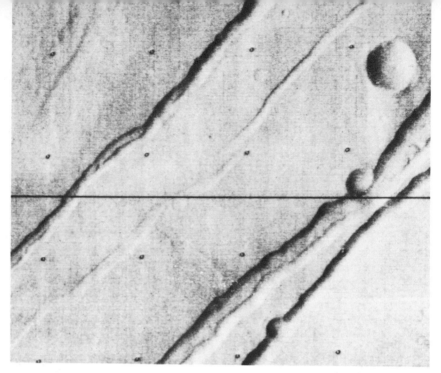

This first clear view of rills or cracks in the Martian crust was taken by Mariner 9, through its telephoto lens, on January 7, 1972. These are generally regarded as tension features. This photo was taken from a distance of 1,072 miles over the Mare Sirenum area of Mars.

But let us look into the far, far future — four billion years or more. If it has managed to survive this long, mankind will find itself in deep trouble. By this time the reactions taking place within the nuclear furnace of the Sun will have caused it to swell enormously. Mercury will be baked. Venus will be fried. The surface temperature of the earth will rise above the boiling point. All life there will cease and all of man's works will disappear. But before this happens, there will be one avenue of escape left open — Mars. There mankind could conceivably cheat extinction for perhaps a few thousand more years. After that, who may foresee what other stepping-stones man will have found to preserve his race?

And so Mars, the planet now thought to be a world possibly without life, may well become the abode of future life — one far beyond the dreams of Schiaparelli and Percival Lowell.

Mars Oct 27 - 1924

Luminous extension at the terminator 14^{h}15^m

15^{h}0^m 15^{h}50^m 16^{h}10^m 16^{h}30^m

In this sketch made by Van Biesbroeck in October of 1924, a cloud is shown at the terminator of Mars.

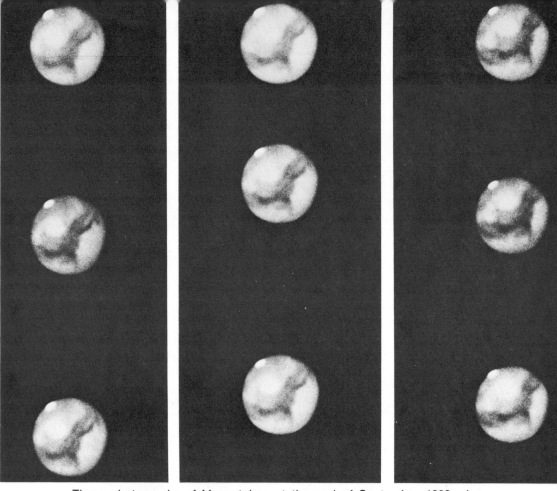

These photographs of Mars, taken at the end of September 1909, show changes due to the planet's rotation. Area is Syrtis Major.

Two view of Mars taken with the 200-inch telescope. Left photograph was taken in blue light; right, in red.

INDEX

ABOUT THE AUTHOR

David Knight, who is Science Editor of a New York publishing house, is an expert in his field. Among his other science books: *The Science Book of Meteorology, Johannes Kepler and Planetary Motion, Copernicus: Titan of Modern Astronomy.*

In this revised edition, he clearly presents all the latest finds–plus the known facts–about the planet Mars. With much previously published material now out-of-date, Mr. Knight says, "Unless someone finds little green men in those photographs, this should be the definitive work".